Anonymous

Trinity Parish Cook Book

Anonymous

Trinity Parish Cook Book

ISBN/EAN: 9783744781220

Printed in Europe, USA, Canada, Australia, Japan

Cover: Foto ©Lupo / pixelio.de

More available books at **www.hansebooks.com**

TRINITY PARISH COOK BOOK.

Choice and Tested Recipes

CONTRIBUTED BY THE

LADIES OF TRINITY CHURCH.

EDITED AND PUBLISHED BY THE

LADIES PARISH AID SOCIETY.

WILMINGTON, DEL.:
THE JOHN M. ROGERS' PRESS,
1892.

Copyrighted according to the Act of Congress, in the year 1892, by
JOHN M. ROGERS, FOR THE "LADIES' PARISH AID SOCIETY," OF
WILMINGTON, DEL.

TRINITY CHURCH, WILMINGTON, DEL.
As designed by Theophilus P. Chandler, Jr., Architect.

TRINITY PARISH.

Organized 1638.   Incorporated 1759.

RECTOR—REV. H. ASHTON HENRY.

WARDENS—HORACE BURR, M. D.,   CHAS. M. CURTIS.

VESTRYMEN—J. PARKE POSTLES,   THOS. F. BAYARD,
ISAAC C. PYLE,   JAMES CARROW,
WM. MONTGOMERY,   SAM'L C. BIDDLE,
JNO. P. R. POLK,   JOHN S. GROHE,
EDWARD T. CANBY.

SEC'Y, JOHN S. GROHE.   TREAS., EDW. T. CANBY.

List of Members of Ladies' Aid Association.

MRS. HENRY R. BOYNTON,   MRS. GEO. LEMAISTRE,
MRS. E. T. CANBY,   MRS. WM. T. MANSLEY,
MRS. MARK M. CLEAVER,   MRS. J. C. MORROW,
MRS. CHAS. M. CURTIS,   MRS. MARGARET McCREA,
MRS. HENRY C. CONRAD,   MRS. HENRY B. NONES,
MRS. PETER B. COOPER,   MRS. GEORGE W. ORTLIP,
MRS. CLELAND,   MRS. ISAAC C. PYLE,
MRS. JOS. L. CARPENTER,   MRS. WALTER PYLE,
MRS. JAMES A. DRAPER,   MRS. J. PARKE POSTLES,
MRS. VICTOR DU PONT,   MRS. F. L. PATTERSON,
MRS. ADELINE L. DORR,   MRS. J. M. ROGERS,
MRS. CHAS. L. DOUGHTEN,   MRS. JOSEPH SWIFT,
MRS. ALEXANDER EVES,   MRS. J. D. SISLER,
MRS. JOHN C. FARRA,   MRS. S. T. TURNER,
MRS. JOHN S. GROHE,   MRS. JAMES A. TAYLOR,
MRS. HORACE W. GAUSE,   MRS. WM. J. WILLIAMS,
MRS. JNO. M. HARVEY,   MISS MARY BURR,
MRS. T. C. HATTON,   MISS CLARA BURR,
MRS. H. ASHTON HENRY,   MISS MARY FARRA,
MRS. H. C. JONES,   MISS K. FARRA,
MRS. TILGH. JOHNSTON,   MISS R. A. GALLAGHER,
MRS. JAMES B. JEFFERIS,   MISS SIDNEY HAYES,
MRS. WM. M. KENNARD,   MISS CARRIE JOHNSTON,
MRS. WM. H. LLOYD,   MISS MARY LAFFERTY,
MRS. PAUL LUKENS,   MISS ANNA PURDY,
MRS. MILO LOCKE,   MISS SOPHIE WAPLES.
MRS. MARGARET LYNDALL.

OLD SWEDES' CHURCH, WILMINGTON, DEL.
ERECTED IN 1698

TABLE OF CONTENTS.

BREAD, &c.

Bread,	17	Pocket Book Rolls,	24
Boston Brown Bread,	34	Potato Rolls,	21, 32
Corn Bread,	25	Quaker Rolls,	36
Indian Loaf,	35	Very Fine Rolls,	31
Baking Powder Biscuit,	21	Rusks,	18, 22, 37
Maryland Biscuit,	22	Mother's Rusks,	28
Burlington Buns,	26	Corn Cake,	33, 34
Germantown Buns,	39	Flannel Cakes,	30
Laplanders,	37	Johnny Cake, (Bishop Williams,)	27
Sally Lunn,	26, 40		
Spanish Buns,	28	Oatmeal Cakes,	29
Muffins,	33	Squash Cakes,	36
Corn Muffins,	35	Pone,	27, 38
Yorkshire Muffins,	19	Yeast,	23
Parker House Rolls,	20		

BREAKFAST AND LUNCH DISHES.

An Egyptian Dish,	54	Duck Terrapin,	59
Beef Steak a la Mode,	57	Egg Dishes,	41, 42, 43, 46, 58
Beef Steak Stewed,	60	Fish Croquettes,	175
Beef Riseroles,	53	Lamb Chops,	44
Boston Baked Beans,	48	Meat Cakes,	46
Cheese Dishes,	49, 50, 54, 56	Omelettes,	42, 44
Chicken Jellied,	53	Oyster Croquettes,	176, 177
Chicken dressed as Terrapin	50	Potato Croquettes,	177
Chicken or Veal Jellied,	52	Potato Puff,	57
Chicken Croquettes,	173, 174, 178	Salmon Timbale	51
		Terrapin Hash,	45
Corn Oysters,	55	Turbot,	52
Curry Gravy,	55	Veal and Ham Moulded,	47
Dressed Calf's Head,	49	Veal Loaf,	45, 59

FISH AND OYSTERS.

Lobster a la Newburg,	69, 70, 71	Terrapin,	71, 72
New Orleans Court Bouillon,	62	Deviled Oysters,	65
		Oysters a la Baltimore,	68
Rock or Cod Fish, (Fresh.)	64	Oyster Pie,	65
Scalloped Halibut,	61	Pickled Oysters,	66
Scalloped Fish,	63	Scalloped Oysters,	67

SOUPS.

Corn Soup, ... 75	Ox Tail Soup, ... 77
Gumbo Soup, ... 75	Potato Soup, ... 73
Mexican Bean Soup, . . . 76	Tomato Soup, . . . 74, 76, 78

SALADS AND DRESSINGS.

Chicken Salad, ... 79	Cabbage Dressing, ... 83
Cold Slaw, ... 81	Chicken Salad Dressing, 85, 86
Crab Salad, ... 80	Mayonnaise Dressing, . . . 83
Potato Salad, ... 82	Salad Dressing, ... 84

PICKLES, CATSUPS, &c.

Green Tomato Pickles, . . 90	Mustard Tomatoes, ... 94
Mangoes, ... 98	Chili Sauce, ... 95, 96
Oil Pickles, ... 88	Shirley Sauce, ... 94
Spanish Pickles, ... 89	Tomato Catsup, . . 91, 95, 96
Cold Catsup, ... 93, 97	To Pickle Onions, ... 87
Cucumber Catsup, ... 92	To Pickle Cucumbers, . . . 88
Hidgeon Catsup, ... 92	

PUDDINGS, CUSTARDS, &c.

Ashburton Pudding, . . . 108	Snow Pudding, ... 104
Baked Indian Pudding, . 101	Suet Pudding, ... 102
Bird's Nest Pudding, . 107	American Cream, . . 111, 116
Carrot Pudding, ... 100	A Nice Frozen Dessert, . . 114
Charlotte a la Royale, . . 104	Apple Custard, ... 110
Chocolate Pudding, . . 106	Bavarian Cream, ... 109
Cottage Pudding, ... 105	Charlotte Russe, ... 116
Dandy Pudding, ... 107	Chocolate Cream, ... 111
Delicate Pudding, . . . 103	Coffee Jelly, ... 115
Delicious Pudding, . . . 102	Cream Meringue, ... 114
Fig Pudding, ... 103	Gelatine Custard, ... 110
French Pudding, ... 109	Hamburg Cream. 112
Fruit Pudding, ... 99	Lemon Custard, ... 113
Hasty Pudding, ... 106	Russian Cream, ... 118
Orange Pudding, . . . 100	Snow Ball Custard, . . . 117
Orange Float, ... 112	Spanish Cream, . . . 113, 117
Plum Pudding, ... 108	Tapioca Cream, ... 115
Queen of Pudding, . . . 101	Fairy Butter (hard sauce), 119
Rice Pudding (without eggs), ... 105	Lemon Butter, . . . 118, 119

PASTRY.

Cream Pie, ... 124	Lemon Pie, ... 123, 124
Egg Pie, ... 120	Mince Pie (Meat), ... 121
English Fruit Pie, ... 123	Pie Crust, ... 122
Lemon Cream Pie, . 121, 122	

CAKES.

Angel Food, ... 143	Layer Cake Custard, . . 163
Black Cake, ... 144	Lemon Jelly for Layer Cake, ... 162
Caramel Cake, ... 134	
Chocolate Cake, . 129, 133, 150	Lemon Cake, ... 128, 129
Cream Cake, 145, 146, 155, 156	Mahogany Cake, ... 127
Cookies, ... 135, 150, 154	Marble Cake, ... 158
Crullers, . . 131, 134, 159, 165	Minnehaha Cake, 147, 148, 149
Composition Cake, . . . 153	Nut Cake, 137, 138, 139, 142
Delicious Cake, ... 142	Orange Cake, . . 128, 131, 151
Doughnuts, . . 126, 132, 163	Pound Cake, ... 126
Feather Cake, ... 152	Puff Cake, ... 161
Fruit Cake, . 136, 140, 141, 160	Sand Tarts, ... 135
Gingerbread, ... 133, 137, 143, 151, 157, 164	Scotch Cake, ... 132, 140
	Spice Cake, ... 166
Harrison Cake, ... 155	Sponge Cake, . . 130, 136, 161
Hermits, ... 160	Straw Cake, ... 147
Jelly Cake, ... 153, 158	Sugar Cakes, ... 148
Jumbles, 127, 130, 145, 152, 159, 162, 164, 165	Victoria Cake, ... 146
	White Mountain Cake, 125, 154

CONFECTIONS AND PRESERVES.

Chocolate Caramels, . . . 169	Ginger Peaches, ... 172
Crystallized Pop-Corn, . . 169	Plum Sauce, ... 171
Everton Taffy, ... 168	Preserved Water Melon, . 170
Marron Glaces, ... 167	Sweet Pickle Plums, . . 172
Pop-Corn Balls, ... 168	Rules for Canning Fruit, . 179
Brandied Peaches, ... 171	

BEVERAGES.

Blackberry Cordial, . . . 181	Grape Wine, ... 181, 183
Egg Nog 180	Grandmother's Whips, . . 182
Elder Blossom Wine, . . 182	Raspberry Vinegar, . . . 183
Dinner Giving, . . . 184-190	Introduction to Sick Room, 195
The Table, ... 191	Household Hints, ... 198
Invalids' Fare, ... 192	

CONTRIBUTORS.

Mrs. J. T. Burrowes,
Mrs. J. L. Burtnett,
Miss Clara A. Burr,
Miss Mary S. Burr,
Miss S. C. Bye,
Miss Lillie Carpenter,
Mrs. Clark,
Mrs. Ellen S. Coffin, Boston,
Mrs. Frances E. Coleman,
Mrs. Peter Cooper,
Mrs. Draper,
Mrs. A. du P.
Mrs. A. P. Eves,
Miss Mary M. Farra,
Mrs. C. H. Gallagher,
Miss Reba A. Gallagher,
Mrs. John S. Grohe,
Mrs. Kate H. Hamilton,
Mrs. J. M. Harvey,
Miss Hayes,
Mrs. Wm. Hearne,
Mrs. H. Ashton Henry,
Miss C. Johnston,
Mrs. M. A. Lloyd,
Mrs. M. M. Lyndall,
Mrs. M. M. McCrea,
Miss E. P. McKrin,
Mrs. E. E. Mansley,
Mrs. S. R. Nones,
Mrs. J. W. Osborne,
Mrs. A. Pyle,
Mrs. M. W. Pyle,
Mrs. Jno. M. Rogers,
Mrs. Aug. Sampson, Boston,
Mrs. Alice Burr Shepard,
Mrs. Stone, Boston,
Mrs. L. G. Sweet, Boston,
Mrs. S. T. Turner,
Miss E. Turner,
Miss Sophie Waples,
Mrs. I. P. Wickersham,
Mrs. E. S. Winslow.

REV. H. ASHTON HENRY,
Rector of Trinity Parish.

Trinity Parish.

THE history of Trinity Parish begins in 1638, when one Peter Minuit built a fort on the north side of Minquas Creek, at a place called by the Indians, "Hopokahacking," naming it Christina, after the then reigning queen of Sweden.

With him came the Rev. Reorus Torkillus as pastor of the colony, afterwards followed by several other priests. For many years religious services were held within the fort, and the churchyard or cemetery was located on a hillside in the rear of the present Church of the Holy Trinity, (Old Swedes).

In 1667, a timber church was built on the south side of the creek on land now owned by Richard Jackson, near the old Alrich house, called Crane Hook, to which the services were transferred, and continued to be held down to the year 1697.

Mr. Biörk, the rector from 1697 to 1714, says in his diary:

"On the 30th of July, (1697) agreeable to notice given on the 25th, we met to choose certain discreet persons from both sides of the River to act for the whole church in selecting and agreeing upon a place where we, in Jesus' name, should set the new church : and from this side were chosen Charles Springer, John Numerson, Hans Pieterson, Hendrick Juarsson and Brewer Seneke ; from the other side, Mr. Wholley Stobey, Staffen Juranson, Jacob Van de Ver and Olle Fransen. And the fixing of the site was earnestly discussed, as some wished it to be Cranehook, some Thirdhook and some Christina ; while those on the East side of the River feared that if they were to contribute to the building of a new church on this side they would not be helped by their brethren when they should be numerous enough to form a separate church on the other side. But they on this side immediately satisfied them by promising them that whenever they should become sufficiently numerous to form a separate church, and able to support a separate minister of the evangelical doctrine, they would do as much for them as they now would do towards building a church on this side of the river. Then those who usually cross over from the other side to Sandhook (New Castle), and come up on this side, thought it would be hard for them to pay ferriage across the Christina Creek if the Church were set on the north side of it, and to content them, it was promised that they should be provided with a new canoe for their own special use in coming to church. And so it was finally unanimously decided that the church should be at Christina, and as there was not ground enough in the cemetery on which to set the building, without encroaching upon graves, and also that it was too much of a side hill, John Stalcop, of his own free will, gave land enough to set the upper half of the church on, and also 20 ft. on each side of the building, and a church-walk to the highway."

It was first decided that the church should be 30 ft. long and 12 ft. in height, and the walls of stone 3 ft. thick, but when they came to the final consideration of the matter Mr. Biörk says:

"Now although some of the Church Wardens wished to have the church no longer than was first talked of, and most of the congregation thought it would be large enough, I opposed it earnestly, in the confidence that God would help me, for I saw plainly that it would not be what it ought, and that we should so build that it would not be necessary to enlarge, and I urged that our contract should be for a building 60 ft. long and 30 ft. broad within the walls, and that the wall should be 20 ft. high and 3 ft. thick, up to the lower end of the windows, and then two ft. upwards, and the contract was so made."

The limited space allotted to this sketch precludes

the recital of the interesting details of construction, and it must suffice to state that all the labor connected therewith was performed by the members of the congregation. With their own hands they quarried the stones and hauled them on sleds to the building site, they sawed all the boards and timbers in the saw pit, even the nails used were forged by the local blacksmith. The work was steadily prosecuted throughout a rigorous winter; but was happily completed and the church ready for consecration on Trinity Sunday, July 4, 1699.

On September 19, 1698, a meeting of the congregation at Christina was held to choose new Church Wardens; but two of the old were retained for the ensuing year, viz: Charles Christopher Springer and Mr. Wholley Stobey, to whom four were added, viz: Hans Pieterson, Brewer Seneke, John Stalcop, and from the other side of the river, Jacob Van de Ver. From that time to the present appears an unbroken record of the Wardens, or as they were afterwards constituted, Wardens and Vestrymen.

The cost of the first church, reckoning all labor and gifts at the then ordinary prices, was estimated to be £800, Pennsylvania currency. A considerable part of this money necessary for the payment of masons, carpenters, etc. obtained from Philadelphia, was donated by members of the congregation. The balance needed was loaned by John Hanson Stelman, a wealthy Swede residing at Elk River, Maryland, on Mr. Biörk's personal security, £130 of this was subsequently paid by him and when he returned to Sweden donated to the church

"Thus was completed in the year of our blessed Lord, 1699, this substantial church building which shall stand for ages a testimony to future generations of the piety, zeal and perseverance of that humble servant of Christ, but really great man, the Rev. Erick Biörk, of whom it may be truly said that of all the illustrious names who have helped to make our beloved Commonwealth what it is, none should be remembered with greater reverence and gratitude."

In the early days of the church, burial within its walls was considered the highest tribute of respect that could be shown to the departed. Mr. Biörk relates that he buried Church Warden Brewer Seneke under his own seat, and Aaron Johanson in the main aisle. He also tells us that he buried a son, who died here, on the South side of the altar, and when John Hanson Stelman, of Elk River, gave up to the church the note for one hundred pounds, as a special mark of gratitude he was voted a place of burial in the main aisle of the church.

During the time of the Swedish supervision all the regular services were held in that language, but with the coming of Mr. Biörk, in 1697, afternoon services in the English language were commenced. At that time there was no English church in the settlement, and it was not until several years later that one was established in the neighboring settlement at New Castle. The Swedish clergymen who succeeded Mr. Biörk, studied as rapidly as possible the new vocabulary until they were fairly able to preach and conduct all services in the English language. During that period however, down to the time when the Rev. Mr. Girelius assumed the Rectorship, books of instruction issued by the "Society for the Propagation of the Gospel," were in general use, until finally at the withdrawing of the Swedish supervision in 1791, none but a very few old people retained knowledge of the Swedish tongue.

The Church of Sweden had been more directly under the Royal authority than even the Church of England. All its commissions for pastorates were given by Royal authority, the Kings and Queens of Sweden being, indeed, nursing fathers and mothers to the churches in this country, for which they expended a considerable amount of money from their own private exchequers, in sending over ministers, in maintaining assistant or extraordinary ministers, and paying extra salaries to the provosts or commissaries of the churches. The churches or congregations, however, paid their resident pastors, built their own churches, and paid for the passage home of ministers who returned to Sweden.

Following is a list of the Swedish Sovereigns, connected with the settlement—and who thus cared for the spiritual wellfare of their former subjects and their descendants.

1st. Gustaf II. Adolf, the great hero of the Protestant war in Germany; who projected the colony but who did not live to carry out his purpose, having lost his life in the battle of Zutphen.

2nd. Christina, his daughter, and foundress of the Colony, who reigned from 1632 to 1654, when she resigned the crown.

3rd. Carl X. Gustaf, who reigned from 1654 to 1660.

4th. Carl XI. who sent over Rudman, Biörk and Aureen in 1696—and reigned from 1660 to 1697.

5th. Carl XII. The great warrior who sent letters to the churches here while a fugitive in Turkey, after the disasterous battle of Pultova.

6th. Ulrica Eleonora, who reigned from 1718 to 1720 and then persuaded the Swedish Diet to declare her husband king.

7th. Fredrik I—Husband of Ulrica, who reigned from 1720 to 1751.

8th. Adolf Fredrik, who reigned from 1751 to 1771.

9th. Gustaf III—who reigned from 1771 to 1792 and under whose reign the Swedish jurisdiction was discontinued in 1791.

Five years before this time, the Swedish churches had united in sending a letter to the Archbishop, stating that the Swedish language was extinct, and expressing their wish to choose Pastors from the English clergy in this country, but the death of the Archbishop Unander, with other complicating circumstances, had until then hindered Archbishop Uno Von Troil, from laying their request before the King—who now considered it reasonable and gave the Swedish ministers permission to return home. The congregation then successfully petitioned the Legislature of Delaware for an amendment of their charter, allowing them to elect either a Lutheran, or Episcopal clergyman for their Rector. The Swedish churches had heretofore been intimately connected with the Episcopal churches, and several of their pastors had received regular stipends and gifts from the English "Society for the Propagation of the Gospel;" so they naturally turned to the Episcopal Church for their Rector.

The congregation continued to worship in the Old Church, until the fall of 1830, when having built a comfortable house of worship at the corner of Fifth and King streets they removed to it, and never afterward returned to the Old Church as a congregation. It still remained standing in the country, with nothing but a country road approaching to it, over a wet and clayey tract of land; which the Borough of Wilmington refused to keep in repair. The congregation however, held their venerable Old Edifice in affectionate regard, and after a few years repaired it thoroughly. They occasionally held services there, and made efforts to keep up Missionary services, which finally proved fruitful and resulted in the building up of a large congregation.

The Church at Fifth and King Streets, was used as the Parish Church, until 1882, having from time to time, been enlarged; and a comfortable Rectory built adjoining it. The congregation not only sustained the missionary work at the Old Church, but also undertook a missionary enterprise, in what was then known as the Brandywine village. Through the munificence of Alexis I. duPont and his family, this resulted in the building of St. John's Church and the growth of a flourishing congregation in connection therewith.

In 1882, it having become evident to the vestry and congregation, that the interests of the Parish required a removal into a more westerly part of the city, and the building of a new church, more convenient to the congregation, more conducive to its future development, and at the same time more favorable to the growth of the congregation at the Old Church. They accordingly sold the church property at the corner of

Fifth and King Streets, and with the approval of the Bishop and Standing Committee of the Diocese, secured an elegible lot of ground, located at the corner of Delaware Avenue and Adams Street. Upon a portion of this a new Chapel was erected to temporarily serve as a convenient house of worship, until improved financial affairs of the Parish would warrant the vestry in carrying out their determination to build an appropriate church structure.

With its last removal, the congregation so increased that the chapel with a seating capacity for four hundred persons soon proved inadequate to provide for its growing necessities. Its financial condition also became greatly improved through the accession of a number of able and generous members, and it was decided upon July 1st, 1889, to finally carry out the purpose so long and persistently cherished, and to proceed immediately with the erection of the commodious and beautiful church in which the congregation now worship, and which is justly considered to be one of the chief architectural ornaments of the City of Wilmington.

Ground was broken for its construction on September 30th, of the same year, and on May 1st, 1890, the Feast of St. Philip and St. James, the corner stone was laid, with appropriate ceremonies. It progressed rapidly towards completion, and on Thursday, January 29th, 1891, was formally Blessed, and for the first time used for service; the attendant ceremonies on the occasion being conducted by its present pastor the Reverend H. Ashton Henry, the Bishop of Delaware being Celebrant, and the Bishop of New York, the Preacher.

The Church is of the Gothic order of architecture, built upon a design furnished by the architect Theophilus P. Chandler, Jr., of Philadelphia. The walls are constructed of rough dressed Avondale stone, and a low ornamental wall of the same material faces Delaware Avenue and Adams Street. The interior is in full keeping with the outward design, with a seating capacity of six hundred.

Its cost exclusive of the tower and spire, as yet uncompleted, but including the grading of the grounds and the stone walls enclosing the same, amounted in all to $45,568.71.

The speedy and satisfactory manner in which this great work has been accomplished, is due no less to the enterprise and liberality displayed by the Vestry than to the wise and efficient labors of the Rev. H. Ashton Henry, who for the past five years of his incumbency, has been earnest and zealous in all work connected with the Parish. The facts of this are more manifest in a thorough and effective organization,—a new and beautiful Church Edifice,—a large and increasing congregation, and a well attended and admirably conducted Sunday School. In fact the congregation of

Trinity, has reason for congratulation that their affairs spiritually, and financially, were never before in a more promising condition.

Holy Trinity (Old Swedes') Church, and Parish since its foundation in 1697 has, down to the present time, enjoyed the ministration of a long line of clergymen, the names of whom are herein recorded in due succession.

1st. Rev. Magister Erick Biörk, who may be regarded as the actual builder of the church, (by his stimulation of the congregation and by his becoming responsible for its cost.)—from 1697 to June 1714.

2nd. Andrew Hesellius, for awhile coadjutor with Mr. Biörk, from May 3rd, 1713 Rector until 1722.

3rd. Rev. Magister Abraham Lidenius, assistant to Mr. Hesellius for about three years, when he assumed charge of the churches of Raccoon and Penn's Neck Parish, newly organized from the old congregations on this side of the river.

4th. Samuel Hesellius, brother of Andrew, from 1722 to 1731.

5th. Rev. John Enneberg from 1731 to 1742.

6th. Rev. Magister Peter Tranberg, from 1742 to 1748, who died during his rectorship and was buried in front of the chancel.

7th. Rev. Magister Israel Aerelius the author of the history of New Sweden, from 1749 to 1756.

TRINITY PARISH.

8th. Rev. Magister Erick Unanander from 1756 to 1759.

9th. Rev. Magister Andrew Borell, from 1759, till his death in 1768.

10th. Rev. Magister Lawrence Girelius who was assistant to Borell one year, and Rector after his death to 1791, when the Swedish supervision was withdrawn, and who returned to Sweden sometime after May 1791.

11th. Rev. Joseph Clarkson of the Episcopal church, 1792 to 1799 inclusive.

12th. Rev. William Pryce, 1800 to 1812.

13th. Rev. William Wicks, 1814 to 1817 inclusive.

14th. Rev. Levi Bull, 1818 to 1819.

15th, Rev. Richard Hall, 1819 to 1822.

16th. Rev. Ralph Williston, 1822 to 1827.

17th. Rev. Pierce Connelly, 1827 to 1828.

18th. Rev. Isaac Pardee, 1828 to 1835.

19th. Rev. Hiram Adams, 1835 to 1838.

20th. Rev. John W. McCullough, D. D., 1838 to 1847.

21st. Rev. Edwin M. Van Deusen, D. D., 1848 to 1852.

22nd. Rev. Charles Breck, D. D., 1853 to 1870.

23rd. Rev. Wm. J. Frost, D. D., 1871 to 1881.

24th. Rev. Henry B. Martin, M. D., 1881 to 1886.

25th. Rev. H. Ashton Henry, 1887, present Rector.

CHOICE AND TESTED
RECIPES.

CONTRIBUTED BY THE LADIES OF TRINITY PARISH.

WEIGHTS AND MEASURES.

One quart of sifted flour weighs one pound.
One pint of soft butter (well packed), weighs one pound.
Two teacupfuls of granulated sugar weigh one pound.
A common-sized tumbler holds one-half pint.
Four teacupfuls equal one quart.
Four tablespoonfuls are equal to one-half gill.
Sixteen ounces make one pound.
A common-sized wineglass holds one-half gill.
One tablespoonful of granulated sugar weighs one ounce.
Two teaspoonfuls of flour, sugar or meal, equal one tablespoonful.
One tablespoonful of soft butter weighs one ounce.
Soft butter the size of an egg weighs two ounces.
Eight tablespoonfuls of liquid equal one-half tumblerful.
Two tablespoonfuls contain a fluid ounce.
Ten medium-sized eggs weigh one pound.
Four gills make one pint.
Two pints make one quart.
Four quarts make one gallon.

# Trinity Parish Cook Book.

BREAD, &c.

BREAD.

MAKE a sponge of two cups of flour, two good sized potatoes, boiled and put through a colander, one cup of good yeast; when light add two teaspoonfuls of sugar, a piece of lard the size of an egg, salt, and flour sufficient to knead well, put to rise again, and when light make into loaves and let rise once more before baking.

Mrs. A. P Eves.

RUSKS.

ONE large coffee cup of warm milk, one cup of sugar, three eggs, two ounces of butter. Melt the butter in the milk, add the sugar and a small quantity of the flour, then the eggs well beaten, dissolve yeast cake in a little milk, and then enough flour to knead into a soft dough. When light make into forms. Let rise about two hours.

Mrs. J. M. Harvey,

YORKSHIRE MUFFINS.

ONE pint of milk, three eggs, one cupful of butter and lard mixed, one cupful of yeast or half of an yeast cake, a very little salt. Warm the butter, lard and milk, then sift in a little flour, beat in the eggs and yeast, continue to add flour until the sponge is soft. Set away in warm place to rise. When light, add flour enough to handle on board, then put back into the bowl and let it get very light. When light, take out bits and roll on board about size of a small saucer, and half an inch thick, put in pans to lighten, then bake. When baked, set upon edge to cool, if not wanted at once to eat. These will keep in a tight box for a long time, and are good, either warmed up or broken apart and toasted.

Kate H. Hamilton.

PARKER HOUSE ROLLS.

TAKE two quarts of flour, make a hole in the centre and put in one tablespoonful of white sugar, butter the size of an egg, one pint of milk that has been boiled but is now cold, one-half cup of yeast, stir this up and let stand over night, in the morning knead well for fifteen minutes, set to rise until two o'clock then roll out and cut round, put a small bit of butter in one half, and double the other half over, put in the baking pans and stand until teatime, this makes three dozen.

Mrs. C. H. Gallagher.

BAKING POWDER BISCUIT.

MIX three heaping teaspoonfuls of baking powder thoroughly, with one quart of sifted flour, add one large spoonful of lard, one teaspoonful of salt, and cold water, or sweet milk enough to mix soft. Bake in a quick oven. Be careful not to work more than necessary in mixing the ingredients together.

Mrs. J. L. Burtnett.

POTATO ROLLS.

TWO cups of mashed potatoes, one half cup of lard, one tablespoonful of sugar, one teaspoonful of salt, one egg, one cup of yeast. Make into a sponge.

Mrs. J. S. Frohe.

RUSKS.

MAKE a sponge of two teacups of milk, one cup of yeast, one-half pound of flour, one-half pound of sugar, one-half pound of butter. Then when very light put flour enough to knead; when light make out in shape. Flavor with cinnamon.

E. Turner.

MARYLAND BISCUIT.

SEVEN cups of the best flour, one cup of lard, one and one-half cups of cold water, and salt; beat until very light. Bake in a quick oven.

Mrs. A. P. Eves.

YEAST.

PARE, and boil eight large potatoes in four quarts of water, when nearly done add one pint of strong hops. When the potatoes are done put through a colander, and strain the water through a bag over them, then add one cup of sweetning either sugar or molasses, or both, one-half cup of salt and one large spoonful of ginger, stir all together, when cool add one cup of rising, let it stand in a warm place twenty-four hours to ferment then bottle and cork up tight, keep in a dark place. This makes about one gallon.

Mrs. Hayes.

YEAST.

ONE quart of grated (raw) potatoes, one cup of sugar, one-half cup of salt, one gallon of boiling water and a few hops.

Mrs. J. S. Frohe.

POCKET BOOK ROLLS.

HAVE ready a quart of sponge about half past eight in the morning; warm a pint of sweet milk with a large piece of butter and lard in it; add salt and four teaspoonfuls of sugar; put in enough sifted flour to make a stiff batter; let it rise in a warm place until it is very light, which will be about twelve; then add enough flour to make it a nice soft dough, knead well and put to rise again; it ought to be light at four, then take a part out and lay it on a floured board; roll it lightly rather thin and cut out with a biscuit cutter; have some melted butter in a tin and with a feather brush the half of the top, then lay the other half over and draw it out a little, pat it down some; lay them in a buttered pan, not to close and let them rise again before baking.

Mrs. A. P. Eves.

CORN BREAD.

TWO-THIRDS of a pint of rice after it has been boiled. Three eggs, one tablespoonful of butter and lard mixed, two teacups of white corn meal, one teaspoonful of Royal yeast powder and enough milk to make as thin as batter cakes, salt. Bake in earthen pans or muffin pans, if in the latter, should not be so thin. To mix take the hot rice, add butter, then the eggs, (yolks) meal, and thin with the milk. Then the whites stirred in with yeast powder. Quick oven is required.

F. R. Howes.

BURLINGTON BUNS.

RUB a half pound of sugar and six ounces of butter into two pounds of flour, and one gill of yeast. Let it rise in a warm place and add one pint of warm milk. Make into cakes; let rise and bake twenty minutes.

Mrs. M. M. McCrea.

SALLY LUNN.

ONE and one-half pounds of flour, one-fourth of a pound of butter, one pint of milk, four eggs, one-half cup of yeast or three-fourths of a yeast cake. Bake in gem pan.

M. A. Lloyd.

PONE.

ONE cup of boiled rice, five ounces of lard, one teacupful of meal, one pint of milk, five eggs, two teaspoonfuls of Royal or three of Rumford's yeast powder. Bake an inch thick, in a dripping pan, and cut into squares.

Mrs. J. W. Ashorne.

JOHNNY CAKE (BISHOP WILLIAMS).

ONE cupful of corn meal, one cupful of flour, one cupful of sugar, one cupful of sour cream (or one cupful of sweet milk, three tablespoonfuls of butter), one teaspoonful of cream of tartar, one half teaspoonful of soda, two eggs, not beaten.

Clara A. Buss.

SPANISH BUNS.

SIX ounces of butter, one pound of sugar, three-quarters of a pound of flour, four eggs, one cup of cream and one of currants, two teaspoonfuls of baking powder; beat together the butter, sugar and yolks of eggs, then add the cream, beat it in; add the flour with the baking powder sifted through it, then the whites of the eggs beaten light; when well mixed add your flavor.

Beat all well together, and add the currants, bake in a quick oven in flat tins twenty minutes.

Mrs. M. W. Pyle.

MOTHER'S RUSKS.

ONE pint of milk, two cups of sugar, one cup of butter, one egg.

Mrs. J. S. Frohe.

OATMEAL CAKES.

ONE cup of boiled oatmeal, one tablespoonful of butter, one quart of flour, one tablespoonful of white sugar, one and one-half cups of milk, one-third teaspoonful of salt, half a cup of yeast (or one-third of an yeast-cake.)

Let the oatmeal be nearly cool before using. Stir all together for eight or ten minutes. Let it rise over night. Fill gem pans three-fourths full, let them rise half an hour. Bake in a hot oven.

Mrs. L. G. Swett,
Boston.

FLANNEL CAKES.

BEAT the yolks of two eggs light; add about one quart of buttermilk or sour milk, salt, two teaspoonfuls of baking soda, and flour enough for a thin batter; lastly, add the whites of the eggs, beaten light.

Mrs. A. P. Eves.

FLANNEL CAKES.

ELEVEN ounces of flour, two good-sized spoonfuls of Rumford's yeast powder; sift together; two eggs, beaten separately, one pint of milk, one and one-half ounce of lard.

Mrs. L. W. Ashorne.

VERY FINE ROLLS.

ONE pint of new milk poured hot over two large potatoes boiled and mashed, two ounces of butter, and two of lard, stirred into the potatoes and milk, a teaspoonful of sugar, one of salt, two pounds of sifted flour, and half a cake of compressed yeast, knead all together for twenty minutes after breakfast if for tea ; when very light, roll them out an inch in thickness, cut, put in pans, rise again until very light, and bake in a hot oven.

Mrs. M. W. Pyle.

POTATO ROLLS.

ABOUT 9 p. m., beat up two eggs, one-half cup of sugar, one cup of mashed potatoes, three-fourths of a cup of melted lard, one cup of warm water, a little salt, a pint of yeast, and two cups of sifted flour. The next morning work up about as stiff as bread dough, and let it rise until noon or a little later. Then roll out about one-half an inch thick, and cut out with a biscuit cutter. Lay one piece on top of another in pans. Let it rise again before baking.

Mrs. J. D. Burtnett.

CORN CAKE.

ONE pint of milk, one-half pint Indian meal, four eggs, a scant tablespoonful of butter, salt, and one teaspoonful of sugar. Pour the milk *boiling* on the *sifted* meal, when *cold*, add the butter (melted), the salt, the sugar, the yolks of the eggs and lastly the whites, well beaten. Bake half an hour in a hot oven.

Mrs. Jno. M. Rogers.

MUFFINS.

ONE pint of milk, two eggs, one large tablespoonful of lard, eleven ounces of flour, two teaspoonfuls of Rumford's yeast powder.

Mrs. L. W. Osborne.

BOSTON BROWN BREAD.

ONE heaping cup of Indian meal, one heaping cup of Garham flour, one heaping cup of rye flour, one cup of sour milk, one cup of sweet-milk, two-thirds of a cup of molasses, one egg, heaping teaspoonful of soda, little salt. Steam four hours, set in oven fifteen minutes. Currants are an addition.

Mrs. Augustus Sampson,
Boston.

CORN DODGERS.

ONE pint of milk, two pints of meal, two eggs, one teacupful of lard, two teaspoonfuls of Royal or three teaspoonfuls of Rumford's yeast powder.

Mrs. L. W. Ashorne.

INDIAN LOAF.

TWO cups of sweet milk, one cup of sour milk, two cups of Indian meal, one cup of flour, four tablespoonfuls of syrup, one tablespoonful of butter, one teaspoonful of soda, one-half teaspoonful of salt. *Steam* from three to five hours.

Mrs. Jno. M. Rogers.

CORN MUFFINS.

ONE cupful of white corn meal, two cupfuls of flour, one half cup of sugar, one half cup of butter, two eggs, one teasponful of soda, two teaspoonfuls of cream of tartar; mix with cold water and bake in a quick oven.

Mrs. A. P Eves.

QUAKER ROLLS.

MAKE a stiff sponge of three pints of milk and three tablespoonfuls of yeast; put to rise over night; then add a half pound of lard, three-quarters of a cup of white sugar, salt and flour enough to work light; let rise again; make out and put in pans to rise before baking.

Mrs. A. P Eves.

SQUASH CAKES.

ONE cup of squash, one-third cup of sugar, one cup of milk, one-third cup of butter, one teaspoonful of soda, two of cream of tartar, two and one-half cups of flour; bake in rings.

Mrs. Augustus Sampson, Boston.

RUSKS.

ONE cup of butter, one egg, one pint of milk, one pint of yeast, and three cups of sugar. Make a sponge at night; in morning make a soft dough and let get light. Mould in forms and bake a light brown.

These rusks dried and grated make a fine Panado for the sick.

Mrs. M. M. McCrea.

LAPLANDERS.

ONE pint of sweet milk, one pint of wheat flour, two eggs, a tablespoonful of melted butter, a little salt. Beat the yolks and whites separately and thoroughly. To be baked in gem pans, which must be heated on top of stove before using, and have the oven hot. Make a nice dessert by cutting a slit in the side and filling with the following cream: One egg, beaten; two small spoonfuls of corn starch, one cupful of milk. Let it become cold before using. Eat with sauce.

S. S. Turner.

CORN PONE.

ONE quart of corn meal, one teaspoonful of salt, two tablespoonfuls of butter; put together in a pan, and pour on enough boiling water to wet them all through. Then add milk until it is a batter, next two teaspoonfuls of cream of tartar, yolks of six or eight eggs beaten well, then the whites beaten to a froth, and one teaspoonful of soda dissolved in milk. Stir all together, and bake in a moderate oven for thirty minutes. This quantity is better if baked in two cakes.

Mrs. J. L. Burtnett.

GERMANTOWN BUNS.

QUARTER pound of butter, half a tumbler of milk, half a pound of white sugar, three-quarters of a pound of flour, four eggs, well beaten, one and a half cups currants, one yeast powder (Bringhurst's), spices. Melt the butter in the milk, add the sugar, then the eggs, then the currants; beating constantly. Then the flour, which should be sifted, and have one grated nutmeg and a tablespoonful of cinnamon mixed with it. Dissolve the blue paper of yeast powder in brandy, the white in rose water or milk; add them separately, beating well all the time, and bake immediately in shallow tin pans.

Mrs. A. du P.

SALLY LUNN.

ONE egg, one-quarter cup of sugar, four tablespoonfuls of melted butter, one cup of milk, two and one-half cups of flour, two teaspoonfuls of baking powder. Beat the eggs, add the butter, then sugar and milk, then flour and baking powder (sifted). Bake in gem pans in hot oven about twenty minutes.

A. Pyle.

BREAKFAST AND LUNCH DISHES.

EGGS WITH OYSTERS.

TAKE three oysters to each egg, and cook them in their own liquor. Strain all the juice off, and chop very fine. Stir into scrambled eggs. Pepper, and salt, and a *very* small portion of nutmeg.

Frances E. Colman.

EGGS WITH CHEESE.

INTO scrambled eggs stir, while on the fire, a half teaspoonful of grated cheese for each egg, and a little parsley chopped very fine. Salt, and a *very* little red pepper. This is a good way to use up old, dry cheese.

Frances E. Colman.

TOMATO OMELETTE.

ONE tablespoonful of tomato sauce to each egg. Three eggs makes a nice dish. Beat eggs separately; add tomatoes to yolks. Then stir in beaten whites very carefully and put in oven. Put pepper and salt to yolks.

Mrs. F. Ashton Henry.

SOFT BOILED EGGS.

PUT the eggs on in cold water, and as soon as the water boils take the eggs out.

M. A. Lloyd.

DEVILED EGGS.

FOURTEEN eggs, two tablespoonfuls of vinegar, two tablespoonfuls melted butter, salt, black and red pepper to taste. Mustard enough to lay on the end of a knife an inch from the top, nine stalks of parsley, chopped fine. Boil eggs about twenty minutes until quite hard. After they have cooled, cut each in half. Remove the yolk and rub until smooth, then mix in the ingredients, after which mould into balls sufficient to fill each half egg.

S. C. Dye.

VEAL OMELETTE.

FOUR pounds of veal cutlet, one-half pound of raw salt pork chopped very fine, beat up four eggs, a cup of rich sweet cream, stir both separately into the chopped meats, melt half pound of butter with some thyme and parsley chopped fine, put it into the meat. Season the whole well with pepper and salt. Bake, slow, four hours, in a round tin. Cut cold for tea or lunch.

Sophie Waples.

LAMB CHOPS.

LAMB chops cooked in this way are excellent. Put them in a frying pan, with a very little water, so little that it will boil away by the time the meat is tender; then put in lumps of butter with the meat and let it brown slowly; there will be a brown, crisp surface, with a fine flavor.

Mrs. M. M. McCrea.

TERRAPIN HASH.

CUT lamb or veal in pieces the size of an olive, being careful to take off all the fat, dust with flour. Have ready a sauce-pan with one-sixth of a pound of butter, half a pint of water, one-half dozen cloves and two hard boiled eggs, chopped fine; throw in your meat and, when scalding hot, add a glassful of sherry or madeira, and half a teaspoonful of Worcestershire sauce. Serve very hot.

Mrs. Jno. M. Rogers.

VEAL LOAF.

THREE pounds of veal chopped fine, one-quarter pound of pork, chopped, three eggs, three tablespoonfuls of milk, one tablespoon of salt, one of pepper, twelve tablespoonfuls of crushed cracker. Mix thoroughly, form into a loaf, and bake, basting occasionally.

S. C. Dye.

STUFFED EGGS.

SIX hard boiled eggs cut in two, take out the yolks and mash fine; then add two teaspoonfuls of butter, one of cream, two or three drops of onion juice, salt and pepper to taste. Mix all thoroughly, and fill the eggs with this mixture; put them together. Then there will be a little of the filling left, to which add one well beaten egg. Cover the eggs with this, and then roll them in bread or cracker crumbs, fry a light brown in hot butter.

M. A. Lloyd.

MEAT CAKE.

THREE pounds of lean beef chopped fine, three eggs, six crackers rolled fine, four tablespoonfuls of milk, six teaspoonfuls of sage, six teaspoonfuls of salt, two and one-half teaspoonfuls of pepper, a small piece of butter, bake two hours.

Mrs. C. H. Gallagher.

VEAL AND HAM MOULDED.

CUT one pound of raw veal, and one-half pound of raw ham into slices and put in a sauce-pan with just enough water to cover. Simmer one hour, put three sprigs of parsley in, chopped fine, five minutes before taking from the fire. While it is cooking, soak one-half ounce of gelatine in a cup of cold water and add with the parsley, cut three hard boiled eggs into slices. Butter a mould and put in the eggs so that they will adhere to the butter, and line the sides and bottom of the mould. Let it set all night and turn out into a dish.

Mary S. Benn.

BOSTON BAKED BEANS.

PICK over a quart of pea beans, wash and soak over night in plenty of cold water. In the morning put into a kettle on the back of the stove, pour on a tea kettle of boiling water and let them stand twenty minutes. Prepare a half pound of fat pork; put into a cup one even teaspoonful of dry mustard, two teaspoonfuls of salt, two tablespoonfuls of molasses; mix well and fill cup with boiling water; pour over the beans, which have been placed in the pot with pork in the centre, fill the pot with boiling water, cover and bake eight or ten hours.

Mrs. Ellen S. Coffin.
Boston.

CHICKEN CHEESE.

BOIL two chickens (in as little water as you can) until tender, then chop fine, season with salt, pepper and a little butter; put a little gelatine in the water the chickens were boiled in; pack the chopped chicken in a jelly mould; pour the gravy over; eat cold.

Mrs. C. H. Gallagher.

DRESSED CALF'S HEAD.

SOAK the head two or three hours in cold water, then take the brains out and tie them up in a cloth; boil the head until it will fall apart, boiling the brains at the same time. When cool pick up, taking out all gristle and skin; chop the meat with four hard boiled eggs; then melt one-half pound of butter in a pan, add the calves head, brains, and eggs, season with salt and pepper, and flavor with sherry wine.

CHICKEN DRESSED AS TERRAPIN.

BOIL a pair of large chickens tender. Then shred them in small pieces and put them in a covered stew pan with one-half pint of boiling water. Rub together until very smooth one tablespoonful of flour, one pound of butter, and the yolks of two eggs, add them to the minced chicken, one-half at a time, stirring very hard. Season with salt and pepper. Let it simmer for ten minutes, then stir in one gill of wine and serve hot.

A. Pyle.

CHEESE PUDDING.

SIX ounces of cheese, grated; two eggs, beaten light; one ounce of butter, one teacupful of milk beaten up together. Bake until like a custard pudding. Salt, pepper and a little mixed mustard to taste. Melt the butter.

Mrs. Deaper —

SALMON TIMBALE.

TAKE one can, or two pounds of fresh salmon, remove the skin, bones and oil, if canned salmon is used. Flake the fish with a silver fork till very fine, then add one tablespoonful of finely chopped parsley, and one teaspoonful of lemon juice, one teaspoonful of salt and one of pepper. Now stir in two tablespoonfuls of *thick* cream and three well beaten eggs. Turn into well buttered timbale moulds, stand in a pan of boiling water, and cook gently in the oven for twenty minutes; then turn from the moulds and serve with a cream or mushroom sauce.

Mrs. Jno. M. Rogers.

TURBOT.

TAKE a white fish or pike, boil until the bones come out easily, sprinkle with salt and pepper. Heat a pint of milk and thicken with enough flour to make it creamy. When cool, add two eggs and quarter of a pound of butter. Season with a dash of onion and parsley. Put in a baking dish, a layer of fish, then a layer of the cream, till all is used, cover with bread crumbs. Bake half (½) an hour.

Mrs. Jno. M. Rogers.

TO MAKE JELLIED CHICKEN OR VEAL.

BOIL the meat till it falls from the bones; use just as little water as possible; when cold, chop it very fine, season with pepper and salt, and a pinch of curry if you like that flavor. Then put it in a mould with a layer of hard boiled eggs, either chopped or sliced. Boil the water in which the meat was cooked until it is half boiled away, and pour it over the chicken; this will be ready for use the day after it is prepared.

Mrs. M. M. McCrea.

BEEF RISEROLES.

TAKE cold beef, either roast or steak, cut off the gristle and chop the beef very fine. To one cupful of meat, add one cupful of stale bread crumbs, one egg, well beaten; salt and pepper to taste; a little allspice, one small onion, chopped fine, with two tablespoonfuls of milk. Roll in balls and fry in boiling lard. Trim the dish with parsley.

Mrs. A. du P.

JELLIED CHICKEN.

BOIL a chicken in as little water as possible until the meat can be easily picked from the bones. Manage to have a pint of the liquid when done. Pick meat from bone in small pieces, removing all gristle and bone. Skim fat from liquor, add one ounce of butter, little pepper and salt, and one-half package of gelatine. Put chicken in a mould, wet with cold water, when gelatine is dissolved, pour liquor over the chicken, turn out when cold. Gelatine should be dissolved in a little cold water, then added to liquor.

Mrs. L. G. Swett.
Boston.

AN EGYPTIAN DISH.

TAKE some thick stewed tomatoes, nicely seasoned with pepper, salt, sugar and onion juice. Do not *sweeten* with sugar, but just enough to correct the acid of the tomatoes. Put a thick layer in the bottom of a baking dish. Have ready enough cold mutton, chopped very fine, and well moistened with gravy, and seasoned well. Make the next layer of this; then put another layer of tomatoes, which ought to fill up the dish. Cover with bread crumbs and with some small bits of butter, and brown in the oven.

Frances E. Coleman.

CHEESE STRAWS.

THREE ounces of grated cheese, two ounces of flour, yolk of one egg, two tablespoonfuls of water, a little salt and red pepper. Roll one-quarter of an inch thick, cut in strips a finger long, and bake a light brown in a moderate oven. N. B.—Before baking, sprinkle with grated cheese (Parmesan is best). If baked the day before, put in the oven for a moment before using, to make crisp.

Mrs. Draper.

CURRY GRAVY.

FRY in butter a sliced onion and two sliced apples. When getting brown, sprinkle over them two teaspoonfuls of curry powder, and one of flour. Let it brown well and add enough boiling water to make a nice gravy. Strain through a fine strainer, and season with salt to taste. Nice dishes can be made of this gravy by putting into it cold beef or mutton, or hard boiled eggs, which have been cut in slices.

Frances E. Coleman.

CORN OYSTERS.

SCRAPE the corn from the cob. To every pint of pulp add two well-beaten eggs, one tablespoonful of flour, one tablespoonful of milk and one half teaspoonful of salt. Fry in hot lard or dripping.

Mrs. Peter Cooper.

CHEESE STRAWS.

THESE straws, which are nice with salad or with after dinner coffee, are easily made. Take one-half of a pound dried flour, one-quarter of a pound of butter, one-quarter of a pound of grated cheese, a saltspoonful of salt, and a little mustard and red pepper. Rub the butter into the flour; then mix all the ingredients well together. Beat the whites of two eggs with one-quarter of a pint of cold water, and stir in enough to form a firm paste. Knead the paste well, and roll it out an eighth of an inch thick, and cut it into straw like strips five inches long. Bake in a quick oven till of a pale brown color. They will keep fresh a long time if closely shut up in a tin box.

Frances E. Colman.

POTATO PUFF.

TWO cups of cold mashed potatoes, two tablespoonfuls of melted butter, beaten to a cream; one egg, beaten light; one cup of milk, salt to taste. Bake in a deep earthen dish, in a quick oven, till nicely browned.

S. C. Dye.

BEEF STEAK à la MODE.

PUT a pound of beefsteak, cut about an inch thick in a chafing dish, in which two tablespoonfuls of butter have been melted, with two or three slices of lemon. Let it cook slowly five or ten minutes; then pour over it a gill of good stock, or the same quantity of hot water, in which a dessertspoonful of "Johnston's Fluid Beef" has been dissolved, also a gill of port wine. Allow the whole to simmer slowly ten minutes longer. When ready to serve, squeeze the juice of a lemon over the steak. A shallow earthen pan can be used on the stove in place of a chafing dish.

(CATERER.)

BEAUREGARD EGGS.

FIVE eggs, one-half pint of milk, one tablespoonful of corn starch, lump of butter, size of a walnut, five squares of toast, salt and pepper to taste. Put eggs on to boil in hot water; let boil for twenty minutes. Take off the shell, chop the whites fine and rub the yolks through a sieve. Do not mix them. Now put the milk on to boil, rub the butter and corn starch together, and add to the boiling milk. Now add the whites, salt and pepper. Put the toast on a hot dish, cover it with a layer of this white sauce, then a layer of the yolks, then the remainder of the whites, and then the remainder of the yolks. Sprinkle the top with a little salt and pepper, stand in the oven for a minute or two and serve.

Mrs. F. Ashton Henry.

DUCK TERRAPIN.

TAKE the remains of cold duck, add two parboiled sweet breads. Cut the duck and sweet breads into dice. Season well with parsley, salt and pepper. Add one cupful of white sauce, stir over hot water until hot. Then add the yolks of two well beaten eggs and a glass of sherry.

VEAL LOAF.

TO three pounds of lean, raw veal, take one pound of salt pork, both chopped finely; one cupful of cracker crumbs, three eggs, pepper and salt. Mix well and make into a loaf. Slap it well, so as to make it solid. Put in a covered pan, sprinkle cracker crumbs over the top, and pieces of butter, (no water). Bake two hours. Eat cold, cut in slices.

STEWED BEEF STEAK.

PUT a steak into a sauce pan with a cup of water. Add a can of tomatoes, an onion in which are stuck a dozen cloves, and a little salt. Let it stew gently (not boil) for six hours. Then take the steak out of the sauce pan and lay it on a hot dish to keep warm. Take out the onion, and beat up the gravy smooth. Add any salt it may require, also pepper, and a little sugar to correct the acid of the tomatoes. It should be served very hot. After dinner chop very fine what is left of the steak, carefully keeping out any fat or gristle, and mix with all the gravy what is left. Season well, and add a little powdered cloves, and allspice, and nutmeg. Measure this mixture, and add the proper quantity of Coxe's Gelatine. Put in a mould and set in a cold place. It can be turned out and sliced for tea.

Frances E. Coleman.

FISH AND OYSTERS.

SCALLOPED HALIBUT.

FOUR pounds of halibut cooked in salt water for half an hour. Put in colander, strain and pick all bones and skin from it. Then put fish in bowl and work with silver fork very fine. Put on range one quart of milk to boil, and in it a very small onion, and let it boil for two minutes; then take half of a pound of butter, three tablespoonfuls of flour, mix thoroughly until perfectly smooth: stir this into boiling milk (first take out onion), cook for a few minutes, until thickened; salt and red pepper to taste. Butter a dish, then put in a layer of fish, then a layer of sauce, and so on until the dish is full; put sauce on top, then fine cracker crumbs, and squeeze a lemon over all. Bake in oven for half an hour and serve hot. This can be put in small fish dishes, and many prefer it so. It is very fine.

Mrs. F. Ashton Henry.

NEW ORLEANS COURT BOUILLON.

HAVE ready a large cup of chopped onions, one-half cup of chopped parsley and one quart of tomatoes. Fry the onions in butter, not very brown, then add a cup of water and the tomatoes, which you have peeled and chopped fine, then add parsley and season with cayenne and salt, thicken with a sprinkling of flour, and put in browning enough to make it a rich color. This sauce will take about half an hour to cook, if it cooks away too much add water or more tomatoes.

Into this sauce you place the fish (rock is best) cut in pieces the size for each person and let it stew slowly until the fish is cooked.

Have ready a large flat dish with pieces of toast, upon which you place the fish, then add to the sauce a cup of claret, when it just reaches a boil pour it over the fish and toast and serve immediately.

Mrs. Jno. M. Rogers.

SCALLOPED FISH.

TWO and a half pounds of halibut or cod, boil in a cloth till tender, with a little salt; let cool and then pick to pieces. Grease baking dish with butter, put layer of fish, then dressing with dots of butter, more fish and so on until all is used, the last layer of fish being well covered with grated cheese. Bake in a quick oven until nicely browned.

DRESSING.

Two-thirds of a pint of cream (part milk will do), piece of butter, size of an egg; salt, dash or two of red pepper, small quarter of a teaspoonful of mustard, and sufficient corn starch to make the cream of pap consistency. Have the cream boiling before adding corn starch. While this is hot, add to the fish.

ROCK OR COD FISH (FRESH).
(A Recipe of Delmonico's.)

FOUR pounds of rock or cod fish, boil until tender in water slightly salted; then pick it up fine, taking out bones and skin. Boil one quart of milk with one onion in slices, four cloves and a sprig of parsley; boil until it tastes of the ingredients, then strain and add four tablespoonfuls of flour, made smooth by a little water, salt and a pinch of evergreen. Let it thicken by boiling to the consistency of cream; add a quarter of a pound of butter. Butter a baking dish or patty dishes and put in layers of fish and sauce, cover slightly with bread crumbs and cook half an hour.

Mrs. Draper —

OYSTER PIE.

ONE hundred large oysters, yolks of three eggs (boiled hard), two ounces stale bread (grated), two ounces butter, two teaspoonfuls of flour; chop the eggs very fine and mix with the crumbs, which season with salt, black pepper and a little cayenne. Put the oysters in a stew kettle, season them with salt and pepper; mix the butter and flour together until smooth, and put in with the oysters; place them over a slow fire until the butter melts, then remove them, make a paste, butter the sides of a deep dish, strew the eggs and bread over the oysters. Bake in a quick oven.

E. S. Winslow.

DEVILED OYSTERS.

TWENTY-FIVE fat oysters chopped up; heat their liquor with a half pint of cream; stir in a heaping tablespoonful of flour, rubbed into the same of butter; add, carefully, two well-beaten eggs, some minced parsley, salt and cayenne. Fill scallop or deep oyster shells, and brown lightly.

Mrs. Peter Cooper.

PICKLED OYSTERS.

PUT one quart of oysters on the fire, with a teaspoonful of salt; let them heat, and as soon as the ears begin to curl, strain and put in cold water; pour the juice into the kettle and add three or four blades of mace, a teaspoonful of whole pepper and allspice, and two tablespoonfuls of best vinegar. Let this boil for five minutes, then pour, boiling hot, over the oysters, add three tablespoonfuls of sherry and keep in a cool place. If you prefer them a little more cooked, keep on the fire a little longer at the first heating, but if done too much they will be soft.

Mrs. Draper

SCALLOPED OYSTERS.

SCALD two dozen oysters in their liquor; drain and return the liquor to the fire with a pinch of nutmeg, a tablespoonful of cream, a tablespoonful of flour and a tablespoonful of butter; shake until thickened, put in the oysters, season with salt, cayenne and butter. Butter a dish, sprinkle with crumbs, fill with the oysters and sauce, sprinkle crumbs over the top, and brown in a quick oven.

Mrs. Peter Cooper.

OYSTERS à la BALTIMORE.

TAKE twenty-five oysters, put them on the fire in their liquor, and let them come to a boil, or till they plump, then remove, put into a colander and drain, cut into small pieces into a sauce-pan on the fire, put one large teaspoonful of butter and one teaspoonful of flour, rubbed together; let it come to a bubble; add one cupful of cream, little salt, pinch of mace and cayenne, one grate of nutmeg, one-half teaspoonful of chopped parsley, one squeeze of lemon, one half teaspoonful of celery seed; add to this the oysters, stir all together. Put the mixture either into a baking dish or individual shells, sprinkle fine crumbs over the top and put into the oven to brown.

Mrs. Jno. M. Rogers.

LOBSTER à la NEWBURG.

SPLIT two good sized, freshly boiled lobsters. Pick all the meat from the shells, cut into one inch lengths, place in a sauce-pan on the hot range, with one ounce of butter, season with one pinch of salt, a half saltspoonful of red pepper, adding two medium sized truffles, cut into dice shaped pieces; cook for five minutes, add a wine glass of good Madeira wine. Reduce one half, which will take three minutes. Then put the yolks of three eggs in a bowl, with a half pint of sweet cream, beat well together; add lobster; gently shuffle for two minutes or until it thickens well. Pour into a hot tureen and serve hot.

Mrs. F. Ashton Henry.

LOBSTER NEWBURG.

FOR six or eight persons, use the meat of a lobster weighing about four pounds, or two small ones; four tablespoonfuls of butter, two tablespoonfuls of brandy, two tablespoonfuls of sherry, two teaspoonfuls of salt, one-fourth of a tablespoonful of pepper, a half pint of cream, yolks of four eggs, and a very slight grating of nutmeg. Cut the meat of the lobster into small, delicate slices, put the butter on the stove in a frying-pan and, when it becomes hot, put in the lobster. Cook slowly for five minutes, then add the salt, pepper, sherry, brandy and nutmeg, and simmer five minutes longer. Meanwhile beat the yolks of the eggs well, and add the cream to them. Pour the liquid over the cooking mixture and stir constantly for one minute and a half. Take from the fire immediately at that time and serve in a warm dish. (I think cayenne pepper preferable to black).

Mrs. Draper—

LOBSTER à la NEWBURG.

TWO pounds of cooked lobster, one cupful of cream, yolks of three eggs, one half goblet of sherry (table), salt and cayenne pepper. Put a little butter in a stew-pan (copper preferred), then add the lobster. When very hot, add the sherry and let come to a boil, then pour in the eggs and cream, and stir until it thickens.

Alice Burr Shepard.

TERRAPIN.

BOIL the terrapin till tender, and, after picking out, add one wine-glass full of sherry wine to each terrapin. Reserve one half of the livers.

DRESSING FOR THE SAME.

For each good sized terrapin, mash one half the liver with the yolk of one hard boiled egg, butter the size of an egg, one teaspoonful of flour, one small teaspoonful of mustard, a dust of cayenne pepper, salt to taste, one tablespoonful of rich cream; add this mixture to the terrapin and wine, and let all simmer until it thickens. Serve very hot.

Mrs. M. M. Lyndall.

TERRAPIN.

PUT the terrapin, alive in boiling water and boil fifteen minutes, or until you can pull off the the outer skin and the toe nails. Then put them in fresh boiling water, add a teaspoonful of salt and boil slowly until the shells part easily and the flesh on the legs is quite tender. When done, take out, remove the under shell and let stand until cool enough to handle; then take them out of the upper shells, carefully remove the sand bags, bladders, the thick, heavy part of the intestines and the gall sacks, which are found imbedded in one lobe of the liver, and throw them away. In removing the gall sack, be very careful not to break it, as it would spoil the terrapin. Break the terrapin into convenient sized pieces, cut the small intestines into tiny pieces and add them to the meat; add the liver broken up, also the eggs in the terrapin. Put into a stewing pan with the juice or liquor it has given out while being cut. For one quart of meat, boil six eggs for twenty minutes, mash with cream. Put meat to simmer, add eggs, about three-fourths of a quart of cream or milk, half a pound of butter; season with salt and pepper; madeira wine to taste. Caramel to color. About one dessertspoonful of flour mixed with cream to thicken. Add wine last thing before serving.

E. S. Winslow

SOUPS.

POTATO SOUP.

FOUR good sized potatoes, one quart of milk, piece of onion size of silver quarter, sprig of parsley, stalk of celery, one bay leaf, one tablespoonful of butter, salt and pepper to taste. Put potatoes on to boil in one quart of cold water. When they are half done, drain all the water off, then cover them again with one pint of fresh boiling water. Add the onion, bay leaf, parsley and celery, and boil until the potatoes are done. Put milk on to boil as soon as the potatoes are done, press all through a sieve. Add the butter to them, then the salt and pepper; now pour over the boiling milk. Mix and serve immediately.

Mrs. J. Ashton Henry.

CREAM TOMATO SOUP.

BOIL one quart of tomatoes and two quarts of water one hour. Press through a colander. Add two tablespoonfuls of butter and one tablespoonful of flour (blended) and a teacup of cream. Salt.

Mrs. Peter Cooper.

TOMATO SOUP.

ONE quart can of tomatoes, two heaping tablespoonfuls of flour, one tablespoonful of butter, one teaspoonful of salt, one teaspoonful of sugar, one pint of hot water. Let tomatoes and water come to a boil, rub flour, butter, and one spoonful of tomato together; stir into boiling mixture, add seasoning. Boil all together, fifteen minutes, rub through a sieve and serve with toasted bread.

S. C. Dye.

CORN SOUP.

ONE dozen ears of corn, two pounds of beef, cut corn from cobs. Put meat and cobs into cold water and boil until meat is done. Take out meat and cobs, and add salt and one tomato to the water, then add the corn; boil three-quarters of an hour; then add one pint of milk or cream; after the milk boils, thicken and season to taste.

Cate H. Hamilton.

GUMBO SOUP.

CUT up a chicken as for a fricassee, and fry a light brown in the pot in which you are going to make your gumbo; pour off all the extra lard in which the chicken was fried, and add three pints of water, two quarts of finely cut okra, one pint of tomatoes, two medium sized onions chopped fine, and a slice of ham, cut small; season with salt and cayenne. Boil all three hours, serve with boiled rice. Having put a ladleful of the soup in the soup plate, place a tablespoonful of rice in the centre.

Mrs. Jno. M. Rogers.

MEXICAN BEAN SOUP.

ONE pint of beans soaked all night. In the morning put the Mexican beans into a pot with three quarts of water, a knuckle of veal, and a piece of butter the size of an egg. Season with pepper and salt. Boil six hours. Have ready in the tureen, a lemon sliced, and one egg boiled hard, and chopped fine. Strain the soup and add one-half tumbler of wine.

Sophie Waples.

TOMATO SOUP.

COOK in one quart of water till very tender, one quart can of tomatoes (or eight large sized ones); add one teaspoonful of soda. When the foaming stops, and not before, add one quart of cold milk, season with pepper, salt, and butter, and let it come to a boil. Roll a few crackers very fine and add just before taking the soup from the fire; put a layer of whole crackers buttered on the bottom of the tureen. Pour the soup over them.

Mrs. M. M. McCrea.

OX-TAIL SOUP.

TAKE two ox-tails, cut into small pieces, put them into a pot without water, set them over the fire to brown, then pour on about five quarts of water, add one turnip, one onion, cut in small pieces, some celery, parsley and leek, also a whole pepper, cloves, one can of tomatoes. Let boil three hours. In the meantime brown a cup of flour in the oven or on the stove. Strain your soup, having taken off the grease, and thicken with the brown flour. To this add a wine glass of Sherry or Madeira and a half glass of catsup, salt to taste.

S. R. Jones.

TOMATO SOUP.

ONE quart can of tomatoes, one pint of stock or water (first the best), one tablespoonful of butter, one tablespoonful of corn starch, one teaspoonful of sugar, one-fourth teaspoonful of baking soda, one small onion, one bay leaf, sprig of parsley, salt and pepper to taste. Put tomatoes in a sauce-pan with the bay leaf, parsley, onion and stock or water; let all stew for fifteen minutes, now press them through a sieve fine enough to remove the seeds. Wash the sauce-pan and return the tomatoes to it; put on the fire to boil; rub the butter and corn starch together, and stir into soup when boiling, stir until smooth; now add salt, pepper, sugar and soda. Butter slices of bread and cut in tiny squares, put them in a baking pan, and toast in the oven until a nice brown; add them to the soup just as it is going to the table.

Mrs. F. Ashton Henry.

SALADS AND DRESSINGS.

CHICKEN SALAD.

BOIL three chickens till tender. Pick the meat from the bones and chop fine. Use celery in the proportion of one-third celery to two-thirds chicken. Chop it separately and not quite as fine as the chicken. For a dressing, take one tumbler and a half of vinegar, three teaspoonfuls of mustard, one-half of a cupful of melted butter or oil, the yolks of five eggs, salt and pepper to taste. After beating, heat this dressing over a slow fire, then stir till nearly cold; then mix together, adding three hard boiled eggs, chopped. This dressing is also very nice for chopped cabbage.

Mrs. J. L. Burtnett.

CRAB SALAD.

TAKE the picked meat of twelve boiled crabs. Set this away to become cold, then arrange it on a bed of crisp lettuce, and pour the dressing over it. Work one-quarter of a pound of butter to a cream, then add the well beaten yolks of four eggs, a dessertspoonful of mustard powder, cayenne pepper and salt to taste. Mix these ingredients well together, then stir the mixture over the fire, and add vinegar until it is as acid as you wish it. Continue to stir it until it thickens like boiled custard, then remove it from the fire and set it away to become thoroughly cold. The dressing must not be poured over the salad until the time of serving it.

Clara A. Burr.

COLD SLAW.

SHAVE very fine one-half of a small solid head of cabbage; melt in a pan a piece of butter the size of an egg, stir in it a heaping teaspoonful of flour; when perfectly smooth, add one-half pint of milk, with an egg beaten in it; stir over the fire until very thick and beginning to boil, then *set it off* and stir in the cabbage; when thoroughly incorporated with the sauce, add a little salt and one-half of a cupful of cold vinegar; stir well until all is mixed. Put it in the dish you will serve it in; dust a little pepper over the top and set away. It should be made half an hour before dinner.

Mrs. M. W. Pyle.

POTATO SALAD.

CUT up some cold boiled potatoes in small blocks; add to these some celery cut in pieces about one-half an inch long, then some onion and parsley, chopped fine; season these with pepper and salt. Make a dressing of one teacupful of vinegar, lump of butter the size of an egg; one egg, one teaspoonful of mustard, one teaspoonful of salt, pinch of pepper, one teaspoonful of sugar. Put vinegar and butter on the stove and let it come to a boil, beat the egg very light and add to it a little water, the mustard, pepper, salt and sugar; pour these into the hot vinegar and stir briskly until it begins to thicken; when cold, add two tablespoonfuls of sweet cream. Pour over the salad.

Mrs. J. P. Wickersham.

CABBAGE DRESSING.

FOUR tablespoonfuls of cream, two eggs, a little red pepper, mustard and salt, one tablespoonful of sugar, four tablespoonfuls of vinegar, one tablespoonful of butter. Boil till thickness of cream; pour *hot* over finely cut cabbage and let stand till *cold*.

Mrs. Jno. M. Rogers.

MAYONNAISE DRESSING.

YOLKS of three eggs, one-half teaspoonful of salt, one-half teaspoonful of dry mustard, a little cayenne pepper, one-half bottle of best olive oil, and one-half cupful of vinegar. Beat with Dover egg beater. In summer begin the dressing with a small baked potato. If the dressing be too stiff, add the white of one egg.

Miss E. P. McKim.

SALAD DRESSING.
THAT WILL KEEP.

BEAT four eggs very light; then beat in half a teacupful of salad oil. Have ready the juice of half a lemon, strained; one-half of a cupful of cream in which has been stirred, until free from lumps, two teaspoonfuls of mustard, one teaspoonful of sugar, one teaspoonful of salt, one saltspoonful of black pepper and one saltspoonful of red pepper. After the oil is well beaten into the eggs, add the lemon juice, then the cream, etc., and last, half a cupful of vinegar. You must taste and see if it is sour enough. (I make mine in a thin quart bowl, which I procured for the purpose.) Set the bowl in a tin of hot water and stir well. It must not be left a minute. Stir it well from sides and bottom of bowl, and keep stirring until it thickens well. Then take off and set the bowl in a dish of ice water and still keep stirring until cold. Bottle, and it is ready for use.

Mrs. M. W. Pyle.

CHICKEN SALAD OR MAYONNAISE DRESSING.

FOR one-half of a chicken, take three eggs, two yolks hard boiled, and one yolk raw; mix to a paste, add a dash or two of red pepper, one-quarter of a teaspoonful of mustard (stir these well); then pour in slowly, four tablespoonfuls of the best olive oil, stirring all the time. Should you find this will not be enough dressing for the quantity of meat and celery (one stalk to this quantity of meat being sufficient), you can add more oil—this must be a thick paste; then add vinegar to taste, and should it not be thin enough, a tablespoonful of cream can be used instead of so much vinegar, as some do not care to have it so tart. Salt to taste. Always wipe the celery dry before cutting in pieces one-quarter of an inch thick. The meat should be a little larger. Keep both in a cool place, and do not add dressing until needed. Boiled chicken is usually preferred, but I like roasted chicken or turkey better.

CHICKEN SALAD DRESSING.

FOR one pair of chickens, the yolks of four hard boiled eggs, mashed thoroughly with a gill of salad oil. Add the yolks of four raw eggs, one small teaspoonful of mustard, one-half of a teaspoonful of red pepper, one tablespoonful of flour, one-half teaspoonful of sugar, one gill of vinegar and half a pint of rich cream. Mix all well together and cook until it begins to thicken. When cold, add a teaspoonful of salt and the whites of the four raw eggs. This is also an excellent dressing for lettuce or tomatoes.

Mrs. M. M. Lyndall.

PICKLES, CATSUPS, &c.

TO PICKLE ONIONS.

TAKE the small, round, white onions, peel off their skins, throw them into a kettle of boiling water over the fire. Put in at a time as many as will cover the top; as soon as they look clear, take them out with a perforated skimmer, and lay them on a soft towel folded double. When all are done and quite dry, put them into jars. Put vinegar, sufficient for your onions, over the fire in a kettle, with the following spices: One ounce of horse-radish, one ounce of whole black pepper, one ounce of salt to every quart of vinegar; let it come to a boil, and pour hot over the onions. Fill the jars only three parts full of onions.

Mrs. M. W. Pyle.

TO PICKLE CUCUMBERS.

KEEP them in a strong brine for several days, then put them in a stone pot and pour boiling vinegar over them. Boil the same vinegar seven or eight times, or until the pickles become green and hard, then take sufficient fresh vinegar to cover them, and to each one and one-half gallons, add four ounces of black pepper, four ounces of mustard seed, two ounces of green ginger, two ounces of allspice, and one-half ounce of cloves, four ounces of celery seed, and one-half dozen *small* Mexican red peppers.

Mrs. Jno. M. Rogers.

OIL PICKLES.

ONE hundred small pickles, one pint of onions, one pint of salt, one cup of olive oil, one-half pound of mustard seed, two ounces of celery seed. Slice pickles and onions, salt them and let them stand about six hours, then drain them, mix in other ingredients and cover with cold vinegar.

S. C. Dye.

SPANISH PICKLE.

ONE peck of green tomatoes, two dozen of large white onions, one dozen green peppers. Chop the onions, peppers and tomatoes fine, sprinkle with salt, put this in a bag and let it drain over night. One gallon of good cider vinegar, one ounce of white ginger root, one-half ounce of tumeric, one ounce of radish seed, one ounce of celery seed, one ounce of black mustard seed, one ounce of white mustard seed, one pound of brown sugar, one-half pound ground mustard. Mix all the spices and sugar in the vinegar, then add the tomatoes, peppers and onions, put on the stove and let simmer until thoroughly done. Then put in jars.

Mrs. J. L. Burtnett.

GREEN TOMATO PICKLES.

TO one gallon sliced tomatoes that are just turning white, and have been scalded in salt and water till they are a little tender, mix a tablespoonful of ground pepper, one tablespoonful of mace, one tablespoonful of cloves, one tablespoonful of mustard, one tablespoonful of cinnamon, four tablespoonfuls of white mustard seed, two tablespoonfuls of celery seed, four pods of green peppers, six onions (more to suit taste), one pint of nasturtiums. Chop onions and peppers fine, mix all together with one-half pound of sugar, and cover with vinegar, and simmer together for fifteen minutes; add more tomatoes, if you do not care to have them so rich with spices.

E. S. Winslow.

TOMATO CATSUP.

ONE bushel of ripe tomatoes, prepared by running them through a sieve. This generally makes about four gallons of juice. Then boil down about one-half, and add one pound of brown sugar, one cupful of salt, one quart of vinegar, one tablespoonful of black pepper, two tablespoonfuls of cinnamon, one ounce of cloves, and a little cayenne pepper.

Mrs. J. L. Burtnett.

CATSUP.

ONE dozen of green peppers, one dozen of onions, one-half bushel of fine ripe tomatoes. Cut the vegetables and sprinkle one-half teacupful of salt over them; let stand over night. In the morning put over the fire, let boil until all is thoroughly cooked. Press through a colander; return to the kettle, add one and one-half pints of vinegar, a shred of mace, one ounce of ground cloves, one ounce of allspice, one-half teacupful of brown sugar; let boil until thick as desired. Bottle and cork tightly.

Mrs. M. M. McCrea.

HIDGEON.

ONE-HALF peck of green tomatoes, one large head of cabbage, six green peppers, all chopped; one-quarter pound of mustard seed, one-quarter ounce of whole cloves, one-quarter ounce of allspice, four tablespoonfuls of salt. Cover with vinegar, and sweeten to taste. Boil one hour.

M. A. Lloyd.

CUCUMBER CATSUP.

TAKE three dozens of full-grown cucumbers, eight white onions; peel cucumbers and onions, grate cucumbers and chop onions as fine as possible; sprinkle them with three-quarters of a pint of salt; put all in a sieve and let stand twelve hours, then add one teacupful of mustard seed, one-half teacupful of black pepper. Mix well and put in a stone jar, with strong vinegar; close tightly for three days and it will keep for years.

Mrs. A. P. Eves.

COLD CATSUP.

TAKE one-half peck of tomatoes, peel, cut, and drain six hours, then mash fine with the hand, take out all hard pieces; add one-half cupful of salt, three-quarters of a cupful of mustard seed, white and black mixed; one gill of nasturtium, one good-sized root of horse-radish, two tablespoonfuls of celery seed, two tablespoonfuls of black pepper, one tablespoonful of cinnamon, one tablespoonful of allspice, one tablespoonful of mace, one quart of vinegar. Bottle, not seal.

Mrs. J. M. Harvey,

SHIRLEY SAUCE.

ONE peck of ripe tomatoes, eight green peppers, eight onions, chop all these fine; eight tablespoonfuls of salt, eight tablespoonfuls of sugar, eight teacupfuls of vinegar. Put one ounce of whole cloves and one ounce of ground ginger in a bag. Add to the mixture and let the whole simmer gently four hours.

Mrs. L. W. Ashorne.

MUSTARD TOMATOES.

SLICE some good, solid tomatoes and lay them out singly on a plate; pepper and salt to taste. Take one egg, one teaspoonful of yellow mustard, a small piece of butter, one tablespoonful of sweet cream; vinegar to suit the taste. Beat all together and set over the fire until it boils, stirring well. When done, it should be about the consistency of cream. If too thick when done, add vinegar. Put a spoonful of this dressing on each slice of tomato, and put some slices of hard boiled egg over them.

E. S. Winslow.

CHILI SAUCE.

FOUR dozen of *large* ripe tomatoes; scald, peel and cut into pieces; four green peppers and four red peppers, eight large onions; peppers and onions, chopped fine together; eight small cupfuls of vinegar, eight tablespoonfuls of sugar, four ounces of salt. All cooked together until like preserves, which will take nearly all day. Put in jars and seal very tightly.

Mrs. F. Ashton Henry.

TOMATO CATSUP.

HALF of a bushel of tomatoes, skinned, boiled soft, and mashed through a colander. Three-quarters of a pint of salt, one and one-half ounces of cayenne pepper, one and one-half tablespoonfuls of black pepper, one ounce of cloves (ground), one and one-half ounces of allspice (ground), two and one-half heads of English garlic, skinned, and separated, cut small; one quart of vinegar. Boil until reduced one-third, and bottle without straining.

Mrs. A. du P.

CHILI SAUCE.

TWENTY-FOUR large ripe tomatoes, six green peppers, four large onions, three tablespoonfuls of salt, eight tablespoonfuls of brown sugar, six teacupfuls of vinegar. Chop the peppers and onions very fine. Peel the tomatoes and cut very small. Put all together into a kettle, and boil gently for one hour.

Mrs. A. du P.

TOMATO CATSUP.

ONE bushel of ripe tomatoes boiled until soft, then squeeze through a wire sieve, add one-half gallon of pure vinegar, one pint of salt, two ounces of whole cloves, one-quarter of a pound of whole allspice (tie whole spices in a cloth), one ounce of cayenne pepper, three teaspoonfuls of black pepper, one tablespoonful of mustard seed; mix together and boil until reduced one-half of the quantity. Then bottle.

Mrs. A. P Eves.

COLD TOMATO CATSUP.

HALF-PECK of tomatoes (ripe), chopped fine; two roots of horse-radish (grated), two red peppers, chopped fine; three stalks of celery, one cupful of nasturtiums, one cupful of onions, chopped fine, one teacupful of salt, one cupful of black and white mustard seed, two teaspoonfuls of black pepper, two teaspoonfuls of cinnamon, one teaspoonful of ground cloves, one teaspoonful of ground mace, one cupful of sugar, one quart of vinegar. Mix all together, put in bottles, seal up tight. Ready for use any time.

Clara A. Burr.

MANGOES.

PUT them in brine for ten days, then wipe dry. Put in strong vinegar and water for two days. Make a filling of chopped cabbage with celery, mustard seed and white pepper with enough olive oil to moisten it. Place them in a jar and cover with this mixture: For thirty-three mangoes, one and three-quarter gallons of vinegar, five and one-quarter pints of sugar, three-quarters of a teacupful of tumeric mixed with vinegar, three-quarters of a cupful of mustard seed, three-quarters of a cupful of celery seed, three-quarters of a cupful of white pepper, three-quarters of a cupful of long peppers, three-quarters of a cupful of ground allspice, a little mace and cloves ground, a little ground mustard. Bruise the mustard and celery seed in a mortar; add a root of horse-radish, or ground horse-radish, two or three garlics, cut up. Cover tightly and keep one year.

Mrs. L. W. Ashorne.

PUDDINGS, CUSTARDS AND SAUCES.

FRUIT PUDDING.

THREE cupfuls of flour, one cupful of sweet milk, one cupful of molasses, one cupful of suet, chopped fine; one cupful of raisins (stoned), one cupful of currants, one teaspoonful of soda, one egg, one tablespoonful of ground cinnamon, one teaspoonful of ground cloves. Mix molasses and milk together, add suet, then raisins, currants and spices, a little flour, then soda dissolved in a little boiling water; add rest of flour, and egg lightly beaten.

SAUCE.

One cupful of powdered sugar, one-half cupful of butter, rubbed to a cream; add yolk of one egg, beaten, then the white, and melt over tea kettle; then add one-half sherry-glass of brandy.

Mrs. Jno. M. Rogers.

ORANGE PUDDING.

BOIL one pint of milk. Stir in while boiling, one and one-half tablespoonfuls of corn starch. Add yolks of three eggs, and one-half cupful of sugar. Have ready one-half dozen sliced oranges, sprinkled lightly with sugar. When the custard is done, pour over the oranges. Make a méringue with the whites of the eggs and one tablespoonful of cold water, beaten lightly, and add three tablespoonfuls of sugar.

S. C. Dye.

CARROT PUDDING.

ONE-QUARTER of a pound of chopped suet, one-quarter of a pound of bread crumbs, one-quarter of a pound of grated carrots, one-quarter of a pound of sugar, one-quarter of a pound of raisins, two eggs, one large spoonful of molasses, wine or brandy sauce. Boil two hours.

Alice Burr Shepard.

QUEEN OF PUDDINGS.

ONE pint of fine bread crumbs, one quart of milk, a piece of butter size of an egg, the yolks of four eggs, one cupful of white sugar, the juice and rind of one lemon. Beat the milk and butter, mix well with the bread crumbs, cool; then add your eggs and sugar, well beaten together, flavor, put in the pan and bake. When done spread the top thick with jelly, and over that the whites of the eggs, beaten light, with a cupful of pulverized sugar, then brown lightly.

Mrs. A. P Evis.

BAKED INDIAN PUDDING.

TWO quarts of scalded milk with salt, one and one-half cupfuls of Indian meal, yellow; one tablespoonful of ginger; let this stand twenty minutes. One cupful of molasses, two eggs, a piece of butter the size of a common walnut. Bake two hours. Splendid.

M. A. Lloyd.

DELICIOUS PUDDING.

TWO cupfuls of fine bread crumbs, one cupful of white sugar, five eggs, one tablespoonful of butter, one quart of fresh milk, one-half cupful of jelly or jam; boil the milk and pour while hot over the crumbs, add the butter and half the sugar. When cool, add the beaten yolks of the eggs. Bake in a pudding dish (filling about two-thirds) until the custard is set, then spread over it a jelly or jam. Cover with a méringue made of the beaten whites of the eggs, and the rest of the sugar. Set in the oven to brown. Serve cold.

Mrs. Hayes.

SUET PUDDING.

ONE cupful of suet, one cupful of molasses, one cupful of milk, one cupful of raisins, three cupfuls of flour; cinnamon, cloves and allspice to the taste; one-half teaspoonful of soda. Put into a tight tin mould and boil three hours.

Sophie Waples.

FIG PUDDING.

SIX ounces of suet, chopped fine; half a pound of figs, chopped fine; three-quarters of a pound of bread crumbs, four ounces of moist sugar (brown is best), a little nutmeg, one egg and one cupful of milk. Boil in a mould, four hours.

SAUCE FOR THE SAME.

One cupful of sugar, two tablespoonfuls of butter, one egg, and a champagne-glass of wine. Beat the yolks and whites separately; the latter to a stiff froth. Mix in a bowl. After boiling sugar, butter and wine together, pour over the egg and return all to the saucepan to thicken for a moment over the fire.

Mrs. Draper —

DELICATE PUDDING.

EIGHT eggs, one quart of milk, eight tablespoonfuls of flour, salt; beat the yolks, add the flour, then the milk; last, the whites of the eggs. Then bake.

Mrs. A. P. Evits.

CHARLOTTE à la ROYALE.

ONE package of Nelson's gelatine, one quart of milk, six eggs, one and one-half cupfuls of sugar, pinch of salt, two teaspoonfuls of vanilla. Soak gelatine three hours in a cupful of water. Heat the milk and stir in the soaked gelatine. Pour it, when dissolved, on the yolks and sugar, well beaten. Let it get cool. Beat whites to stiff froth, and add spoonful by spoonful to the congealing "jamse mange," beating steadily until you have a light yellow sponge, flavoring as you work. Line a glass dish with sponge cake, and fill with the sponge, cover with more cake and set on ice until needed.

Mrs. Peter Cooper.

SNOW PUDDING.

ONE pint of boiling water poured over one-half box of gelatine. Stand till cold, and add two cups of sugar, juice of two lemons, whites of three eggs. Beat all together forty-five minutes.

S. C. Dye.

COTTAGE PUDDING.

ONE cupful of sugar, one cupful of milk, two eggs, a lump of butter the size of an egg, two teaspoonfuls of cream of tartar, one teaspoonful of soda, and flour to thicken. Eat hot.

SAUCE.

Beat a tablespoonful of butter to a cream, add one tablespoonful of cream, and sugar enough to thicken.

Mrs. J. D. Burtnett.

RICE PUDDING (WITHOUT EGGS).

TWO quarts of milk, one-half teacupful of rice, a little less than a teacupful of sugar, the same quantity of raisins, a teaspoonful of cinnamon. Wash the rice, and put it with the rest of the ingredients, into the milk. Bake rather slowly, from two to three hours; stir two or three times the first hour of baking.

Mrs. G. P. Wickersham.

CHOCOLATE PUDDING.

TEN tablespoonfuls of grated bread crumbs, eight tablespoonfuls of grated chocolate, one quart of milk. Boil in a farina kettle until pap. Then pour boiling hot over the yolks of six eggs and one teacupful of sugar, stirring all the time. Put in oven and bake one-half hour, covering it. Just before taking out remove cover and brown a little. Beat the whites light, add sugar and vanilla, spread the top, and brown lightly.

Mrs. L. W. Osborne.

HASTY PUDDING.

ONE pint of milk, enough flour to make a thin batter. Bake in cups, twenty minutes.

Mrs. J. S. Frohe.

DANDY PUDDING.

BOIL one quart of milk, sweeten, and flavor with lemon; mix four tablespoonfuls of corn starch in some cold milk. Beat the yolks of three or four eggs, stir into the corn starch and milk; add the whole to the boiling milk, and cook ten minutes. Beat the whites of the eggs perfectly light with eight teaspoonfuls of white sugar and the juice of one lemon; heap this up, in large spoonfuls, over the pudding. Brown, slightly, in the oven.

MRS. A. DU P.

BIRD'S NEST PUDDING.

PARE and core some good cooking apples, boil slightly, and put into a dish with butter, sugar and nutmeg. Make a rich custard, pour over them. Put in the oven and bake.

Mrs. A. P. Eves.

ASHBURTON PUDDING.

ONE cupful of raisins, one cupful of suet, one cupful of molasses, one cupful of milk, three and one-half cupfuls of flour, one teaspoonful of soda. Put in a bag and boil three hours.

E. S. Winslow

PLUM PUDDING.

ONE cupful of milk, a scant cupful of finely chopped suet or lard (or two tablespoonfuls of butter), one cupful of molasses, a scant teaspoonful of soda, a scant teaspoonful of salt, two eggs, one pound of raisins, one-half pound of currants, three cupfuls of flour, two teaspoonfuls of cinnamon and two teaspoonfuls of allspice, one-half teaspoonful of cloves and one-half teaspoonful of mace, one-half glass of wine or brandy. Steam three hours.

Mrs. J. L. Burtnett.

BAVARIAN CREAM.

ONE pint of cream, one tablespoonful of vanilla. Make very sweet and whip together until quite light; then add the whites of three eggs, beaten stiff, and one-half box of gelatine dissolved in water. Put in a mould and put in a cool place.

Mrs. F. Ashton Henry.

FRENCH PUDDING.

PUT a little more than a pint of milk to boil, and while it is coming to a boil, beat the whites of three eggs to a very stiff froth; which put in the boiling milk and turn over, so that both sides will be scalded; then mix one tablespoonful of corn starch with milk, to which add the beaten yolks sweetened, and put in the milk after taking out the whites, and boil to a custard. Place a layer of custard in a dish, then dots of white of the eggs, and a macaroon on each white, and then a layer of custard, alternately.

E. S. Winslow.

APPLE CUSTARD.

THREE cupfuls of stewed apples, nearly one cupful of sugar, six eggs, one quart of milk. Make the stewed apples very sweet, and let it cool. Beat the eggs light and mix with the apples, seasoning with nutmeg only. Then stir in gradually the milk, beating as you go on; lastly add the whites.

S. C. Oye.

GELATINE CUSTARD.

ONE-HALF box of Cox's gelatine, soaked ten or fifteen minutes, in four tablespoonfuls of cold water, then add a pint of boiling water, the juice of two lemons, or one-half cupful of wine, and one cupful of white sugar, strain; when cool, add the well beaten whites of three eggs; mix thoroughly, and place in a mould to cool. To be eaten with a custard made of the yolks of the eggs and one pint of milk flavored with vanilla.

Mrs. A. P. Eves.

CHOCOLATE CREAM.

ONE quart of cream, three ounces of chocolate, five eggs, one teacupful of white sifted sugar. Grate the chocolate into the cream, and scald both together, stirring constantly until it boils. Stand aside to cool. Beat the yolks of the eggs, and one-half the sugar together, add to the cream and beat well together. Beat the whites of the eggs and remainder of the sugar to a stiff froth, spread over the cream, and brown in the oven. Serve cold.

Mrs. Hayes.

AMERICAN CREAM.

ONE quart of milk, four eggs, one-half box of Cox's gelatine. Soak the gelatine in the milk until dissolved, then put on the fire, and when the milk boils, put in the yolks of the eggs, well beaten, with five tablespoonfuls of sugar and one tablespoonful of extract of vanilla; let it boil about five minutes, then stir in the whites of the eggs, that have been beaten stiff, with five tablespoonfuls of sugar. When thoroughly mixed, take off the fire and put in moulds in a cool place. Serve with cream.

Mrs. I. B. Burrowes.

ORANGE FLOAT.

ONE quart of water, the juice and pulp of two lemons, and one coffee cupful of sugar. When boiling, add four tablespoonfuls of corn starch; let boil fifteen minutes, stirring all the time. When cold, pour it over four or five peeled and sliced oranges, and over the top spread the beaten whites of three eggs. Sweeten and add a few drops of lemon.

Mrs. M. M. McCrea.

HAMBURG CREAM.

DISSOLVE one-quarter pound of sugar in the juice of one large lemon, adding the grated rind, then the yolks of five eggs, well beaten, stirring it to prevent curdling. Place it over the fire in a kettle of boiling water, stirring till it gets thick, then add the whites, beaten to a stiff froth; stir in thoroughly. Take off the stove and put into small glasses and set aside to cool.

S. R. Noyes.

LEMON CUSTARD.

ONE lemon, three eggs, one cupful of sugar, one cupful of milk, small piece of butter, two tablespoonfuls of rolled cracker; separate the white from the yolk of the eggs, and beat with three tablespoonfuls of fine sugar. After the pies are baked, cover the top with the icing, and let it get a light brown.

E. S. Winslow.

SPANISH CREAM.

ONE-HALF box of gelatine soaked one-half hour in one pint of milk, stir in the yolks of three eggs, beaten with four tablespoonfuls of sugar; boil again. After the mixture is cold, stir in the whites of eggs beaten to a froth. Flavor with vanilla, and cool in moulds.

Mary M. Fanna.

CREAM MÉRINGUE.

ONE pound of powdered sugar, six eggs (the whites only). Beat whites very stiff. Then carefully put in sugar, a little at a time till all is in, then flavor. Put brown paper, wet on one side, on under side of meat pan, then put one tablespoonful of méringue, a little distance apart, until the paper is covered; sprinkle powdered sugar over each, and brown in oven. These can be eaten as they are, or a little of the inside can be taken out and whipped cream put in, in place of it, putting two méringues together.

Mrs. J. Ashton Henry.

A NICE FROZEN DESSERT.

ONE and one-half pints of cream, the rind of one orange, grated, and the juice of two oranges, one-quarter of a pound of stale macaroons, six ounces of sugar; whip the cream, stir all in and freeze like ice cream.

Mrs. A. P. Eves.

COFFEE JELLY.

ONE-THIRD box of Cox's gelatine soaked in one-third of a cupful of cold water one-half hour; add two cupfuls of strong coffee, boiling hot, and three-quarters of a cupful of sugar; strain and pour into moulds. Serve with rich cream, whipped. Delicious if partly frozen in moulds.

Mrs. Jno. M. Rogers.

TAPIOCA CREAM.

ONE quart of milk, three dessertspoonfuls of Pearl tapioca, two eggs, one-half cupful of sugar. Soak the tapioca in water, over night; in the morning put it with the yolks of the eggs and sugar, in the milk over the fire, until thick, set it off, and when two-thirds cool, have your whites well beaten and stir all together and set on ice, or where it will get cold. Flavor with vanilla.

Mrs. Clark.

AMERICAN CREAM.

ONE-HALF box of gelatine dissolved in one quart of milk, four eggs, beaten separately; five tablespoonfuls of sugar in each part of the eggs. Put the milk on the stove and when it comes to the boiling point, add the yolks of the eggs and sugar. Watch it, and when it comes to the boiling point again, remove and add the whites of the eggs well beaten with the sugar. Flavor to taste, and pour into moulds. It should be made the day before using. I always flavor with vanilla.

Mrs. J. L. Burtnett.

CHARLOTTE RUSSE.

FOUR eggs and one-half pound of sugar, beat well together. Dissolve one ounce of isinglass in one teacupful of milk; whip to a froth one quart of cream; flavor, eggs and sugar with two teaspoonfuls of vanilla; stir all together, then pour into a dish, previously lined with cake.

Mrs. A. P Evis.

SPANISH CREAM.

DISSOLVE one-half box of gelatine in one quart of milk. After standing one hour put it on the stove and let it come to a boil, like custard. Beat the yolks of four eggs with seven tablespoonfuls of white sugar. When the milk and gelatine boil, pour it over the eggs and sugar. Return it to the stove until it is of the consistency of custard. About a minute after removing from the fire, stir in the well beaten whites of the eggs, beating until smooth. Flavor with vanilla. Pour into moulds dipped in water. Eat cold with cream.

S. C. Dye.

SNOW BALL CUSTARD.

ONE quart of milk, sweetened to taste, put on to boil; beat the yolks of eight eggs very light, pour the boiling milk over the eggs and return to the fire; when thickened, pour it through the sieve and let cool; when cold, stir in about one-half pound of macaroons, then beat the whites of the eggs light with pulverized sugar, and spread on top. Flavor the custard with vanilla or bitter almond.

Mrs. A. P Evey.

RUSSIAN CREAM.

SIX eggs, one and one-half pints of milk, one-half box of gelatine, one large cupful of sugar, two wine-glassfuls of wine, or two tablespoonfuls of vanilla. Pour the cold milk over the gelatine and stand in a warm place to dissolve, then stir in the yolks of the eggs, well beaten with the sugar; let it come to a boil, then stir until almost cold, pour in the whites of the eggs, beaten stiff, then the flavoring. Mould and let cool slowly. To be eaten with or without cream.

Mrs. A. P Eves.

LEMON BUTTER.

ONE cupful of water, one cupful of sugar, grated rind and juice of one lemon boiled together fifteen minutes; then add two eggs beaten very light, a piece of butter the size of an egg, and two dessertspoonfuls of corn starch mixed with a little cold water. This makes one pint.

Mrs. Hayes.

FAIRY BUTTER (HARD SAUCE).

A PIECE of butter the size of a walnut; beat to a cream with pulverized sugar; flavor with wine or brandy.

Mrs. J. S. Frohe.

LEMON SAUCE.

TWO lemons, two cupfuls of white sugar, one cupful of butter, six eggs; mix all together in a sauce pan and let come to a boil.

Mrs. J. L. Burtnett.

PASTRY.

EGG PIE.

Put in a baking dish a layer of grated bread crumbs, then a layer of hard boiled eggs cut in slices, and so on, alternately, until the dish is full, ending with the bread crumbs. Put pepper and salt over each layer, both of bread crumbs and of eggs. Lay some bits of butter over the top, and, just before it is put into the oven, pour over it a cupful of milk. Brown nicely. If wanted for breakfast, it can be got ready the night before, and the milk poured over it in the morning.

Frances E. Coleman.

MINCE PIE MEAT.

TWO pounds of beef and suet each, boiled and chopped; four pounds of chopped apples, two pounds of raisins, two pounds of currants, two pounds of sugar, one-half tablespoonful of cinnamon, two nutmegs, one teaspoonful of ground cloves, a little mace and salt, one cupful of molasses, one pound of citron, one pound of figs, chopped; one pint of good wine, one pint of brandy, one quart of cider. Put all on stove (but brandy) until heated through, then take off and, when cool, add brandy.

*Mrs. Stone,
Boston.*

LEMON CREAM PIE.

TAKE the juice and grated rind of one lemon, one cupful of sugar, yolks of two eggs, three tablespoonfuls of flour, milk to fill the plate. Bake with under crust. Put on a méringue of the two whites, two tablespoonfuls of sugar. Bake a light brown.

S. C. Dye.

PIE CRUST.

ONE pound of flour, one-quarter pound of butter, one-half pound of lard, one coffee cupful of ice water. Mix flour and lard together, handle little as possible. Roll out twice with the butter between.

Mrs. Jno. M. Rogers.

LEMON CREAM PIE.

ONE lemon, two eggs, one cupful of milk, one cupful of sugar. Beat the yolks light, add lemon, sugar and milk, a small lump of butter, one teaspoonful of corn starch in the milk; boil until it thickens. When cool, pour into the baked crust. Beat the whites of the eggs to a froth, add one-half cupful of pulverized sugar, put on the top and brown.

Mrs. J. S. Frohe.

LEMON PIE.

ONE lemon, one cupful of sugar, three eggs, lump of butter the size of an egg, one cupful of milk. This makes one pie. Make a méringue of the whites of two eggs, beaten well, and one cupful of pulverized sugar.

S. C. Dye.

ENGLISH FRUIT PIE.

ONE and one-quarter pounds of raisins (seeded), one and one-quarter pounds of suet, one and one-quarter pounds of apples (chopped), two and one-half pounds of currants, one quart of cider, one quart of sherry, one pint of brandy, two and one-half teaspoonfuls of allspice, one teaspoonful of cloves, one teaspoonful of cinnamon, one large nutmeg, one teaspoonful of salt, four cupfuls of brown sugar, the rind and juice of two lemons. Extra brandy added when each pie is baked.

Mrs. Jno. M. Rogers.

CREAM PIE.

For two pies, take one pint of cream or very rich milk, sweeten to taste, boil, then thicken with two tablespoonfuls of corn starch and the yolks of three eggs, mixed well together; flavor with vanilla. Pour this custard in plates, after they have been previously lined with crust. When baked, spread the whites of the eggs beaten light, with pulverized sugar on top. Put in the oven and brown lightly.

Mrs. A. P. Ever.

LEMON PIE.

One cupful of hot water, one tablespoonful of corn starch, one cupful of white sugar, one tablespoonful of butter, juice and rind of one lemon; boil for a few minutes; when cool, add one egg. Bake with under and upper crust.

Mrs. J. M. Harvey.

CAKES.

WHITE MOUNTAIN CAKE.

YOLKS of four eggs, whites of six eggs, three-quarters of a cupful of butter, one cupful of milk, three cupfuls of granulated sugar, four and one-half cupfuls of flour, one tablespoonful of baking powder. Rub butter and sugar to a cream, add yolks of eggs previously beaten, and then the milk. Stir in flour, then the whites of eggs, well beaten, and lastly, the baking powder. This will make two cakes of three layers each.

FILLING.

Whites of three eggs, one cupful of granulated sugar, one-half cupful of water. Make a syrup of water and sugar, and when clear, pour over the well beaten whites of the eggs and beat until cold, then add one teaspoonful of vanilla, and spread between the layers.

A. Pyle.

DOUGHNUTS.

SIX eggs, one quart of milk, two and one-half pounds of sugar, three tablespoonfuls of butter, one teacupful of yeast, three nutmegs, flour enough to roll. Let rise in the evening, cut out and let rise on the board all night.

Mrs. L. W. Ashorne.

POUND CAKE.

ONE and one-half cupfuls of butter, two cupfuls of sugar, seven eggs, one and one-half pints of flour, one teaspoonful of Royal Baking Powder, two tablespoonfuls of rose water and a little grated nutmeg. Rub the butter and sugar to a white light cream, add three eggs, one at a time, and the rest two at a time, beating five minutes between each addition; add the flour, sifted with the powder; then the flavoring, and mix into a smooth batter, and bake in a paper lined cake tin, in a steady oven, fifty minutes to an hour.

E. S. Winslow.

MAHOGANY CAKES.

TWO eggs, beaten very light, separately; put into the yolks one pint of milk, one and one-half pints of flour; stir in the whites, beaten to stiff froth. Put it in cups and bake at once in a very hot oven. The cups must not be greased.

Sophie Waples.

ALMOND JUMBLES.

ONE pound of sugar, one-half pound of butter, one pound of almonds, blanched and chopped fine, two eggs, flour enough to mix stiff. Roll thin. Moisten the top of each one with the whites of eggs and sprinkle with sugar. Bake quickly. Jumbles may be wet with a brush or cloth saturated with sherry wine, after they are cooked, and then returned to the oven to dry.

C. Johnston.

LEMON CAKE.

ONE-HALF cupful of sugar, one teaspoonful of butter, one tablespoonful of milk, three eggs, one cupful of flour, one teaspoonful of baking powder. Bake in jelly tins, and put between, two apples and one lemon grated together, with a little sugar.

M. A. Lloyd.

ORANGE CAKE.

TWO cupfuls of flour, one-half cupful of butter, two cupfuls of granulated sugar, yolks of five eggs, whites of four eggs, one-half teaspoonful of soda, one teaspoonful of cream of tartar, rind and juice of one lemon.

ICING FOR SAME.

Rind and juice of one orange, whites of two eggs, one pound of powdered sugar. Bake the cake in four layers, and after it is quite cold, put icing between each layer and on top.

Mrs. C. H. Gallagher.

LEMON CAKE.

THREE eggs, two cupfuls of flour, one and one-half cupfuls of sugar, one-half cupful of milk, one-half cupful of butter, the juice and grated rind of one lemon. Reserve the whites of the eggs, add to them one-half pound of pulverized sugar. Make icing flavored with lemon. Bake cake in two layers.

Mrs. M. M. McCrea.

CHOCOLATE CAKE.

ONE cupful of butter, two cupfuls of sugar, three cupfuls of flour, one cupful of sweet cream, yolks of seven eggs, and one whole egg, one teaspoonful of cream of tartar, and three-fourths of a teaspoonful of soda, or two teaspoonfuls of baking powder.

ICING.

Whites of four eggs, one pound of sugar. Take two blocks of chocolate out of a cake, put in a tin and place in a pan of boiling water until melted. Then mix it in the icing and spread on cakes, which have been baked in jelly cake tins.

Mrs. J. L. Burtnett.

JUMBLES.

ONE-HALF pound of butter, one-half pound of sugar, one pound of flour, one egg, little nutmeg; roll thin and bake in a quick oven.

Mrs. J. S. Frohe.

VELVET SPONGE CAKE.

TWO cupfuls of sugar, six eggs, leaving out the whites of three, one cupful of boiling hot water, two and one-half cupfuls of flour, one tablespoonful of baking powder. Beat the yolks a little, add the sugar and beat fifteen minutes. Add a cupful of *boiling* water just before the flour. Flavor with a teaspoonful of lemon extract. Bake in three layers, putting between them icing, made by adding to the three whites of eggs, beaten to a stiff froth, six dessert-spoonfuls of pulverized sugar to each egg, and flavor with lemon.

Mrs. M. M. McCrea.

ORANGE CAKE.

THREE eggs, one large cupful of sugar, one-half cupful of milk, two cupfuls of flour, two teaspoonfuls of baking powder, one-quarter of a pound of butter. This will make two nice thick layers, or three, if you prefer.

FILLING.

Grate about one-half of the yellow rind of one orange, peel off all the white, then grate all of the orange and juice with the yellow rind; add one cupful of confectioner's sugar to this. Beat the white of one egg to a very stiff froth, with two tablespoonfuls of sugar. Then stir all together and spread on the cake when it is cold.

E. S. Winslow.

CRULLERS.

TWO cupfuls of sugar, one cupful of butter, three eggs, one teacupful of milk or cream, one nutmeg, flour to roll out, one of Bringhurst's yeast powders. Cut a hole in the middle of each cake.

Mrs. L. W. Ashorne.

SCOTCH CAKE.

ONE pound of butter, two pounds of white sugar, four eggs, four or five tablespoonfuls of cinnamon. Roll *very* thin.

Mrs. L. W. Ashorne.

DOUGHNUTS.

ONE cupful of light bread sponge, one cupful of milk, one cupful of sugar, two eggs, two ounces of butter, one and one-half large spoonfuls of rose water, one-half cupful of yeast, flour to knead. Heat the milk and butter together, add with the sugar to the bread sponge, while warm; then add rose water and eggs, well beaten, and flour. Make them as soft as possible. Let them get very light, then roll about three-quarters of an inch thick, and cut any shape you wish. Let them stand a little while to rise. Fry in boiling lard.

Mrs. Hayes.

GINGERBREAD.

FOUR eggs, one cupful of brown sugar, four cupfuls of molasses, two cupfuls of butter, two cupfuls of milk, one-half teaspoonful of soda, flour to make it the consistency of pound cake. Ginger and spice to the taste.

S. S. Lerner.

CREAM CHOCOLATE CAKE.

THREE-QUARTERS of a cupful of butter, one cupful of milk, two cupfuls of sugar, whites of eight eggs, three cupfuls of flour, two teaspoonfuls of baking powder, and flavor with bitter almond.

ICING.

Three cupfuls of A. sugar, and three-quarters of a cupful of sweet milk, boiled exactly four minutes. Pour into a dish, and beat until cool and thick. Flavor with vanilla and spread on the layers. Then melt one-quarter of a cake of chocolate, and dip in your knife and spread a thin layer over the cream, which will be smooth and hard.

Mrs. J. L. Burtnett.

CRULLERS.

ONE and one-half cupfuls of sugar, one cupful of milk, one teaspoonful of butter, two eggs, two even teaspoonfuls of baking powder, flour to make stiff enough to roll.

Lillie Carpenter.

CARAMEL CAKE.

TWO cupfuls of sugar, one-half cupful of butter, one cupful of sweet milk, three cupfuls of flour, the whites of ten eggs, beaten to a light froth; three teaspoonfuls of baking powder, and one teaspoonful of essence of lemon.

ICING.

Three and one-half cupfuls of brown sugar, and one cupful of rich, sweet cream; put on stove and let boil, until, when tried in water it hardens. Remove from stove and flavor with vanilla.

Mrs. J. D. Burtnett.

SUGAR WAFERS.

THREE-FOURTHS of a pound of sugar (heavy), three-fourths of a pound of flour (light), one-half pound of butter, five eggs, beaten separately; grated rinds of two lemons, one *even* teaspoonful of baking powder. Drop in baking pan with spoon.

Mrs. Jno. M. Rogers.

SAND TARTS.

ONE pound of sugar, three-quarters of a pound of butter, two eggs (reserving one white to wash them with), sufficient flour to roll out without sticking; roll thin and cut out; dust them with sugar and cinnamon, and wash with the remaining white of egg, lay on one or two pieces of shell-bark nuts and bake. Keep dough very cool.

Reba A. Gallagher.

SPONGE CAKE.

EIGHT eggs, three-fourths of a pound of sugar, one-half pound of flour, juice and grated rind of one lemon. Beat the whites of the eggs until stiff; add the yolks one at a time, then beat in the sugar gradually, and then the lemon juice and rind. *Stir* the flour in last. Bake about three-fourths of an hour in a moderate oven.

Mrs. Hayes.

FRUIT CAKE.

ONE pound of butter, one pound and two ounces of flour, one and one-fourth pounds of brown sugar, nine eggs, beaten separately; four good nutmegs, grated; two pounds of seeded raisins, two pounds of currants, one-half pound of citron, cut fine; one-half pound of lemon and orange rind, cut very fine; one-half teacupful of good brandy.

Mrs. J. L. Burtnett.

HARD GINGER CAKES.

THREE pounds of flour, two pounds of sugar, one pound of butter, one gill of cream, four tablespoonfuls of ginger, a very little allspice, one pint of molasses, (not syrup,) roll *very* thin.

Mrs. L. W. Ashorne.

NUT CAKE.

ONE-HALF pound of butter, two cupfuls of sugar, four eggs, one cupful of milk, three cupfuls of flour, one gill of brandy (if desired), one large cupful chopped nuts, two teaspoonfuls of baking powder. Mix butter and sugar to a cream; add eggs and milk. Mix flour, baking powder and nuts together. Put all together, stir thoroughly and bake in a moderate oven one hour.

E. E. Gransley

NUT CAKE.

FOUR eggs, one pound of sugar, four tablespoonfuls of flour, one pint of nuts. Beat the yolks of the eggs, add the whites previously beaten, sugar, flour and nuts; drop in buttered tins and bake quickly.

A. Pyle.

NUT CAKES.

HEAT a pint of milk lukewarm, stir into it one cupful of melted butter, stir in flour to make a thick batter; add one cupful of yeast. Set in a warm place until light. Work in, two and one-half cupfuls of sugar, four eggs, cinnamon and salt. Knead in flour stiff enough to roll; keep in a warm place until it rises again. When light, roll out an inch thick, cut with a wine-glass, let stand fifteen or twenty minutes. Fry in hot lard.

Clara A. Burr.

HICKORY NUT CAKE.

WHITES of twelve eggs, three large coffee cupfuls of white sugar, one coffee cupful of butter, one coffee cupful of sweet milk, five coffee cupfuls of flour, two teaspoonfuls of baking powder, and one pint of nut meat, chopped fine. Bake in layers, as for jelly cake, with icing between, or in a large cake. If baked in a loaf, the cake will be much improved by adding a pound of raisins.

Mrs. J. L. Burtnett.

NUT CAKE.

ONE cupful of butter, two cupfuls of sugar, five eggs, one-half teaspoonful of soda. Dissolve in one cupful of sweet milk, one pound of flour, one teaspoonful of cream of tartar, sifted through flour; one pint of nuts (shell-barks), one pound of raisins (stoned).

Mrs. Jno. M. Rogers.

FRUIT CAKE.

TAKE one pound of brown sugar, one pound of good butter, beaten to a cream; put one pound of sifted flour into a pan; whip eight eggs to a fine froth, and add to the creamed butter and sugar; then take two pounds of cleaned currants, one pound of stoned raisins, one-half pound of citron, one-fourth pound of blanched almonds, crushed, but not pounded, to a paste; one small cupful of molasses, one even teaspoonful of ginger, one teaspoonful of cinnamon, one-half teaspoonful (small) each of mace, nutmeg and cloves, one large wine-glassful of good French brandy. Bake in a slow oven for five hours. This cake will keep a year if it is put in a tin case and covered tightly in an airy place.

Mrs. C. H. Gallagher.

SCOTCH CAKES.

ONE pound of brown sugar, one pound of flour, one-half pound of butter, two eggs, cinnamon, roll very thin to bake.

A. Pyle.

FRUIT CAKE.

ONE pound of butter, one pound of flour, one pound of sugar, two and one-half pounds of seeded raisins, one pound of citron, one and one-half pounds of best dried currants, cleaned and dried; one-fourth of a pound each of preserved orange and lemon peel, ten eggs, and one glassful of currant jelly, one-half pint of brandy, ground nutmeg, cinnamon, cloves and allspice, of each, a sufficient quantity to spice. Caramel (burnt sugar) to darken the color, if desired. Cream the butter and sugar, add the beaten yolks of the eggs; stir well together, add one-half the flour, next the spices and then the whites of eggs, well beaten, with rest of flour; then the brandy; the fruits, the citron, orange and lemon peel should be cut in slips. Finally bake in a slow oven four hours.

Mrs. J. M. Harvey,

NUT CAKES.

THREE eggs, one pound of sugar, one pound of flour, one-half pound of butter. Reserve the white of one egg for spreading over the cakes. Roll the dough very thin and cut with a cutter. Spread the top of the cakes with the white of egg; dust sugar and cinnamon and stick with any kind of nuts.

E. S. Winslow

DELICIOUS CAKE.

THREE eggs, two cupfuls of sugar, one cupful of butter, one cupful of milk, or water, three cupfuls of flour, two and one-half teaspoonfuls of baking powder. Beat the yolks of eggs with sugar till light, then add butter and whites of eggs, well beaten, and lastly, flour and milk.

Mary M. Fanva.

GINGER SNAPS.

TWO cupfuls of molasses, five tablespoonfuls of butter, two tablespoonfuls of cinnamon, one tablespoonful of ginger, one teaspoonful of soda, flour to make stiff enough to roll.

Lillie Carpenter.

ANGEL'S FOOD.

WHITES of eleven eggs, one and one-half tumblerfuls of granulated sugar (sifted four times), one tumblerful of sifted flour, one teaspoonful of vanilla, one teaspoonful of baking powder. Beat eggs to a stiff froth; add sugar lightly, then flour gently, then vanilla. Do not stop beating until put in a pan. Bake forty minutes in a moderate oven. Do not open stove door until the cake has been in fifteen minutes. Use a pan that has never been greased.

S. C. Dye.

BLACK CAKE.

ONE pound of sifted flour, one pound of fresh butter, one pound of powdered white sugar, twelve eggs, two pounds of raisins, two pounds of currants, one pound of citron, two tablespoonfuls of mixed spices, two nutmegs, powdered; one large wine-glassful of wine, one large wine-glassful of brandy, one-half glassful of rose water. Allow twice as much cinnamon as mace, in mixing the spice. Cream the sugar and butter together, beat the eggs very light, stir them in, alternately, with the flour; add gradually the spices and liquors. Stir in the raisins and currants, alternately; they must be well floured. Stir the whole for ten minutes. Line the bottom and sides of a large tin pan with paper, well buttered; put in part of the mixture and then a layer of citron, cut thin, but not too small, and so on until all the mixture is in. Bake four or five hours in a moderately hot oven.

Sophie Waples.

JUMBLES.

ONE pound of butter, one pound of sugar, one and one-quarter pounds of flour, six eggs, flavor with mace, roll in coarse granulated sugar, and flour, and twist.

Mrs. L. W. Ashorne.

CREAM PUFFS.

MELT one-half cup of butter in one cup of hot water. While boiling, beat in one cupful of flour. Take off the stove and cool; then stir in three eggs, one at a time, without beating. Drop quickly on tins, and bake about twenty-five minutes in a moderate oven. Open the side of each puff, and fill with the following

CREAM.

One-half pint of milk, one egg, two tablespoonfuls of flour. Boil the same as any custard, and flavor with vanilla.

S. C. Dye.

CREAM CAKE.
GOOD FOR A DESSERT.

THREE eggs, one cupful of sugar, one cupful of flour, one half teaspoonful of soda, one tablespoonful of milk, one teaspoonful of cream of tartar. Bake in two pie plates, split and spread with warm corn starch flavored.

Mrs. A. P. Eves.

VICTORIA CAKES.

ONE pound of flour, one-half pound of butter, one-half pound of sugar, four eggs, six tablespoonfuls of cream; flavor with almond. Beat the butter and sugar together to a cream; add eggs, cream and flour, and flavoring. Beat all well together and drop from a spoon into a floured tin; sift granulated sugar over them and bake quickly.

Mrs. Hayes.

STRAW CAKES.

TWO cupfuls of sugar, three eggs, one cupful of sour milk, lump of butter the size of an egg, one pint of flour, two teaspoonfuls of cream of tartar, one teaspoonful of soda. Bake in pans, and, when cold, cut in pieces.

Mrs. J. D. Burtnett.

MINNEHAHA CAKE.

ONE-HALF cupful of butter, two cupfuls of sugar, three cupfuls of flour, one cupful of milk, whites of six eggs, one teaspoonful of baking powder, sifted with the flour. Beat the eggs very light. Bake in three layers.

FOR THE FILLING.

Boil two cupfuls of sugar, and one-half cupful of water until it strings like a hair from the spoon, and pour slowly on the beaten whites of two eggs. Mix in one cupful of seeded raisins, and one cupful of English walnuts, and spread between the layers and on top of the cake.

Reba A. Gallagher.

SUGAR CAKES.

THREE eggs, three-quarters of a cupful of butter one and one-half cupfuls of sugar, flavor, one teaspoonful of baking powder, and flour enough to roll out.

Mrs. A. P Eves.

MINNEHAHA CAKE.

TWO cupfuls of sugar, one-half cupful of butter, four eggs, one cupful of milk, flour enough to thicken, about three cupfuls; two teaspoonfuls of yeast powder, the last thing. Bake in layers.

ICING.

Two cupfuls of granulated sugar, one-half cupful of boiling water. Let it boil until sugar is dissolved (do not let it boil too long or it will thicken). Have two eggs, well beaten, and pour the sugar over them, and beat until cold. Use raisins, figs and English walnuts between the layers.

S. C. Dye.

MINNEHAHA CAKE.

ONE-HALF cupful of butter, two cupfuls of sugar, whites of six eggs, one cupful of milk, three cupfuls of flour, three teaspoonfuls of baking powder, and one teaspoonful of vanilla. First, cream the butter and sugar, then add the milk and flour with the baking powder, and lastly, the whites of the eggs, beaten to a stiff froth. Bake in three layers.

ICING FOR THE ABOVE.

Boil two cupfuls of sugar with seven tablespoonfuls of water until it will string from the spoon thin as a hair. Have the whites of two eggs beaten to a froth, and gradually stir in the boiling sugar; add to this one teacupful of seeded raisins and one teacupful of English walnuts and spread on the layers.

Mrs. M. M. Lyndall.

LEMON COOKIES.

ONE pound of butter, one pound of granulated sugar, two pounds of flour, four eggs, one teaspoonful of soda, flavor with lemon.

E. Turner.

SPONGE CHOCOLATE CAKE.

TEN eggs, one pound of pulverized sugar, one-half pound of flour, juice and rind of one lemon.

Beat the yolks of the eggs very light, then mix sugar with flour and flavoring, and lastly, the lightly beaten whites, reserving two of the whites for the icing.

ICING.

One pound of pulverized sugar, with one-quarter of a cupful of water, boiled ten minutes; pour on the well beaten whites of the two eggs until cold. Flavor with chocolate.

Mrs. A. P Eves.

SOFT GINGERBREAD.

ONE egg, one cupful of molasses, one cupful of boiling water, one teaspoonful of ginger, one teaspoonful of soda, one pint of flour, one tablespoonful of butter.

Mrs. J. S. Frohe.

ORANGE CAKE.

ONE-HALF cupful of butter, one and one-half cupfuls of sugar, one-half cupful of water, two heaping cupfuls of flour, whites of four eggs, yolks of three eggs, grated rind and juice of one orange, two teaspoonfuls of baking powder.

FROSTING.

Whites of two eggs, sugar sufficient to stiffen, and the grated rind and juice of one orange.

Mrs. J. L. Burtnett.

PLAIN JUMBLES.

ONE cupful of butter, one cupful of sugar, two cupfuls of flour, two eggs. Stir the butter and sugar to a cream, add a little grated nutmeg and eggs; last, the flour. Drop on buttered tins. Bake quickly in a hot oven.

Mrs. M. W. Pyle.

FEATHER CAKE.

BEAT two ounces of butter, and one-half of a pound of pulverized sugar together until mixed; then add one gill of milk, and beat again until very light. Weigh out one-half of a pound of flour; add one-third to the mixture, and beat again; separate two eggs; beat the whites to a very stiff froth; then beat the yolks until creamy; add them to the mixture; then the whites, then the remaining flour, beating well after each addition of materials. Add one heaping teaspoonful of baking powder, and flavoring. Mix thoroughly, and turn into a well greased cake pan. Bake in a moderate oven, thirty minutes.

Mrs. J. P. Wickersham.

ROLL JELLY CAKE.

THREE eggs, beaten together well; one cupful of sugar, three tablespoonfuls of cold water, pinch of salt, one and one-half cupfuls of flour, two teaspoonfuls of baking powder mixed with the last one-half cupful of flour. Spread with jelly, and roll while warm.

S. C. Dye.

COMPOSITION CAKE.

ONE-HALF of a pound of butter, three-quarters of a pound of sugar, three-quarters of a pound of flour, five eggs, one gill of cream, one wine-glassful of brandy, one wine-glassful of wine, one nutmeg, one pound of mixed fruit. Cream the butter and sugar. Beat eggs light, and add them, then the brandy, spice and wine; then the flour, and lastly, the fruit. Beat hard all the time; bake slowly.

Mrs. A. du P.

COOKIES.

THREE-QUARTERS of a pound of butter. One and one-quarter pounds of sugar, one-half pint of warm water, four tablespoonfuls of caraway seed, one teaspoonful of soda dissolved in water, three pounds of flour. Mix well. Roll very thin and bake in a quick oven.

MRS. A. DU P.

WHITE MOUNTAIN CAKE.

TWO cupfuls of fine white sugar, one-half cupful of butter, one cupful of sweet milk, three cupfuls of sifted flour, whites of eight eggs, two teaspoonfuls of baking powder, and flavor to the taste.

ICING.

Whites of three eggs, beaten to a froth, and then add nine heaping teaspoonfuls of pulverized sugar to each egg; then spread on layers, sprinkling cocoanut between layers, and on top and sides.

Mrs. J. D. Burtnett.

HARRISON CAKE.

SIX cupfuls of flour, one cupful of sugar, one and one-half cupfuls of molasses, one cupful of sour milk, two cupfuls of butter, four eggs, two pounds of fruit, cut very thin (citron), currants, washed and dried; one yeast powder mixed in milk, cream, butter and sugar; add yolks of eggs, beaten light; then molasses and milk; then flour, and lastly, the fruit; beating all the time.

Mrs. A. du P.

ICE CREAM CAKE.

TWO cupfuls of sugar, one-half cupful of butter, one egg, and yolks of two others, one cupful of milk or water, three cupfuls of flour, one teaspoonful of baking powder. Bake in layers. Flavor with vanilla.

ICING.

Let two small cupfuls of pulverized sugar boil with one-quarter of a cupful of water, for about ten minutes. Pour the solution, while boiling, over the beaten whites of two eggs; beat together until cold and smooth, and spread between the layers.

Mary M. Fanva.

FRENCH CREAM CAKE.

CREAM.

BOIL nearly a pint of sweet milk; reserve a small quantity of it to add to the eggs, etc., take two small tablespoonfuls of flour, beaten with the reserved milk. To this add two eggs, whites and yolks; when the milk has boiled, stir this in slowly with one scant cupful of sugar; when almost done, add one-half cupful of butter, or less, if you choose. Flavor with lemon.

CAKE.

Three eggs, one cupful of white sugar, one and one-half cupfuls of flour, one teaspoonful of cream of tartar in the flour, one-half teaspoonful of soda, two tablespoonfuls of cold water. This will make two cakes. Bake in pie pans, quick oven. Split while warm. Spread with cream.

E. S. Winslow

GINGERBREAD.

THREE cupfuls of New Orleans molasses, one and one-half cupfuls of lard, one cupful of sugar, one cupful of sour milk, or buttermilk, two tablespoonfuls of ginger, two tablespoonfuls of baking soda, one egg, a little pinch of salt, and flour enough to roll out. To be baked in a quick oven.

Mrs. A. P Eves.

SOFT GINGERBREAD.

ONE pound of flour, three-quarters of a pound of sugar, one-half pound of butter, four eggs, well beaten, four tablespoonfuls of ginger, one teacupful of milk, one yeast powder (Bringhurst's). Cream the butter and sugar; add the yolks of eggs, well beaten. Dissolve blue paper of yeast powder in milk, the other in water, or wine (about a wine-glassful), add one of these; then mix ginger and flour, and beat them in by degrees; add other half of powder. Bake in flat pans twenty minutes.

MRS. A. DU P.

ROLL JELLY CAKE.

FOUR eggs, one cupful of powdered sugar, one tablespoonful of water, one cupful of flour, one-half teaspoonful of baking powder. Flavor with lemon. Bake in two layers, in a long pan. When baked, spread with jelly, and roll quickly in a napkin.

Mary M. Foura.

MARBLE CAKE.

BLACK PART.

YOLKS of eight eggs and one whole egg, two cupfuls of brown sugar, one cupful of molasses, one cupful of sour milk, one-half teaspoonful of soda, one cupful of butter, four cupfuls of flour, allspice, cinnamon and cloves.

WHITE PART.

Whites of eight eggs, three cupfuls of white sugar, one cupful of milk, one cupful of butter, four cupfuls of flour, one-quarter of a teaspoonful of soda. Mix a layer of the white, and wave the dark around it to represent marble.

Sophie Waples.

JUMBLES.

ONE and one-quarter pounds of flour, one pound of butter, one pound of sugar, three fluid ounces of sherry wine or brandy, three eggs, rose water, if desired. Rub the butter and sugar to a cream; add the wine or brandy and one-third of the flour (if rose water is to be used, add here); then add the eggs, first beaten very light, and another third of the flour; place the mixture in a cold place for two hours, then roll thin and cut, using the third portion of flour to prevent sticking. Bake immediately in a hot oven.

Mrs. J. M. Harry.

CRULLERS.

TWO cupfuls of sugar, four eggs, six teaspoonfuls of melted butter, one cupful of milk or water, spices to taste, three teaspoonfuls of baking powder. Flour enough to roll out.

Mary M. Fanna.

HERMITS.

ONE cupful of butter, one and one-half cupfuls of sugar, one-half cupful of currants, one cupful of chopped raisins (stoned), three eggs, one-half teaspoonful of soda, one-half teaspoonful of all kinds of spices. Flour to make stiff.

Miss E. P. McKim.

LAYER FRUIT CAKE.

ONE cupful of sugar, three-quarters of a cupful of butter, two cupfuls of flour, whites of five eggs, three teaspoonfuls of baking powder. Flavoring to taste. Take from this one large tablespoonful. Bake the rest in two cakes as for jelly cake; to this tablespoonful add one-half cupful each of chopped raisins and citron, flour and molasses, two teaspoonfuls of cinnamon, one-half teaspoonful of cloves, and one wine-glassful of brandy. Bake this in one layer. Put together with soft frosting, putting the fruit layer in the middle. The top may be frosted or not, as you choose.

Mary M. Fawa.

PUFF CAKE.

TWO-THIRDS of a cupful of butter, two cupfuls of sugar, three cupfuls of flour, one cupful of sweet milk, three eggs, two teaspoonfuls of cream of tartar, one teaspoonful of soda. Spice to suit taste.

Mrs. J. S. Frohe.

SPONGE CAKE.

BEAT the whites of five eggs stiff, the yolks of seven eggs as stiff as possible. Beat these together. Put three-quarters of a pound of sugar, and one-half teacupful of water on to boil; then pour over the eggs, beating all the time till quite cold; add lightly one-half pound of flour, vanilla.

Clara A. Buss.

LEMON JELLY FOR LAYER CAKE.

ONE cupful of boiling water, one cupful of sugar, one tablespoonful of corn starch, rind of one lemon, and juice of two lemons.

Mrs. Jno. M. Rogers.

JUMBLES.

THREE-FOURTHS of a cupful of butter, one and one-half cupfuls of sugar, three eggs, three tablespoonfuls of milk, flour to roll, with a teaspoonful of baking powder in it. Roll about one-fourth of an inch thick, sprinkle with granulated sugar, gently roll it in; cut with a hole in the center, and bake.

Mrs. Hayes.

CUSTARD FOR LAYER CAKE.

ONE cupful of milk, two eggs (yolks), one full teaspoonful of corn starch, one heaping tablespoonful of sugar, one-half teaspoonful of vanilla, speck of salt.

Mrs. Jno. M. Rogers.

DOUGHNUTS.

TAKE one pint of milk and one cupful of good yeast; make into a sponge; when light, add one pound of sugar, one-half pound of butter, six eggs, beaten light, one nutmeg, a little mace, and flour to make a stiff dough. Put to rise, and when light, cut out and fry in hot lard.

Mrs. A. P. Eves.

GINGER CRACKERS.

ONE cupful of New Orleans molasses, one cupful of dark brown sugar, one cupful of lard, two tablespoonfuls of ginger, two tablespoonfuls of cinnamon, two teaspoonfuls of baking soda dissolved in three tablespoonfuls of boiling water. Flour to make dough stiff enough to roll very thin.

Mrs. J. L. Burtnett.

CINNAMON JUMBLES.

FOUR eggs, one pound of brown sugar, three-quarters of a pound of butter, one teaspoonful of soda, three tablespoonfuls of ground cinnamon, one heaping quart of flour. Dissolve soda in a tablespoonful of milk. After mixing all together, take a piece of dough the size of a hickory nut, roll long, in crushed sugar; catch both ends together and bake.

E. Turner.

CRULLERS.

STIR together three tablespoonfuls of melted butter and two cupfuls of sugar, add two well beaten eggs, a cupful of sweet milk in which a teaspoonful of soda has been dissolved. Flavor, and flour with two teaspoonfuls of cream of tartar. Roll out and fry in hot lard.

Mrs. A. P. Eves.

RICH JUMBLES.

RUB one pound of butter into one and one-quarter pounds of flour. Beat four eggs with one and one-quarter pounds of sugar, and when very light, beat in two tablespoonfuls of rose water and two tablespoonfuls of brandy. Then add to the flour and butter, and set out in the cold to stiffen. Roll in rings, and bake in a steady oven. Sift powdered sugar over them.

Mrs. J. D. Burtnett.

SPICE CAKE.

YOLKS of four eggs, one cupful of butter, one cupful of sour milk, two cupfuls of flour, two cupfuls of sugar, one teaspoonful of soda, one small nutmeg, one tablespoonful of cloves, one tablespoonful of cinnamon, a pinch of salt. Can be baked as a layer cake, and use the whites of the eggs for an icing.

Mrs. A. P Evey.

CONFECTIONS.

MARRON GLACÉS.

REMOVE the outer skin of the chestnut and boil them until tender, though not till they are in the heart mealy; then skin and dry on a cloth. To a pound of loaf sugar, add one-quarter of a pint of water and boil for a few minutes, then lay in the chestnuts, turning them once or twice with a fork. Take them out of the sugar and run a large needle with a thread through them and hang them up to dry.

Mrs. Jno. M. Rogers.

EVERTON TAFFY.

ONE-QUARTER of a pound of butter; soon as melted add one pound of brown sugar. Stir gently.

E. Turner.

POP CORN BALLS.

TWO cupfuls of molasses, one-half cupful of sugar, piece of butter size of nutmeg. Boil till it hardens when dropped in cold water; take off the stove and stir in, briskly, five quarts of pop-corn. Mould into balls.

Mary S. Bunn.

CHOCOLATE CARAMELS.

THREE pounds of brown sugar, one and one-half cakes of Baker's chocolate, one-half pound of butter, two cupfuls of milk. Flavor with vanilla. Boil one-half hour.

E. Turner.

CRYSTALLIZED POP-CORN.

ONE cupful of sugar, one tablespoonful of butter, three tablespoonfuls of hot water. Boil until it hardens in cold water. Take off the stove and stir in three quarts of pop-corn; stir until they separate and crystallize.

Mary S. Burr.

PRESERVES.

PRESERVED WATER MELON (DELICIOUS).

TAKE the part of melon which lies between the rind and core, boil in clear water, with a teaspoonful of alum, and grape leaves over the top, for two or three hours, or until transparent; then lay in cold water, changing it as it becomes warm. Take out of water, weigh, and wipe it dry. Make syrup pound for pound, with one-quarter of a pound of root ginger; cut in thin slices, also four lemons, sliced. Put in the melon and boil until you can run a splint through it. Place in jars, boil the juice ten minutes longer, or until it becomes a thick syrup; intersperse the ginger and lemon before pouring over the syrup. Put papers dipped in brandy over jars. Set away for use.

S. R. Howes.

PLUM SAUCE.

ONE peck of plums, six pounds of sugar, one ounce of cinnamon, one ounce of cloves, and one gill of vinegar.

Mrs. J. D. Burtnett.

BRANDIED PEACHES.

TO every pound of fruit, add one-half pound of sugar. Prepare fine white cling peaches; after syrup is made, put in the fruit, cook until tender, but not broken, take out carefully, place in jars, removing all juice. After the juice is boiled to a thick syrup, let cool, and to every pint, add two-thirds of a pint of white preserving brandy. After standing for a day, the jars can be filled up, if necessary.

S. R. Innes.

GINGER PEACHES.

TWELVE pounds of pared peaches, six pounds of sugar, one pint of vinegar, two ounces of white Jamaica ginger. Boil sugar and vinegar together, and pour *over* the fruit. Let stand over night boil next day all together.

A. Pyle.

SWEET PICKLE PLUMS.

TWELVE pounds of plums (Damsons), eight pounds of brown sugar, one pint of vinegar. Wash the plums, put all into the kettle together, boil until thick; skim off the seed, add a few cloves. Stir all the time.

Sophie Waples.

CROQUETTES.

CHICKEN CROQUETTES.

ONE chicken, one-quarter of a pound of butter, one-quarter of a pound of flour, one cupful of chicken broth, one cupful of milk, four yolks of eggs, parsley, nutmeg, red pepper, black pepper and a little salt. Chop the parsley very fine, and put it with the butter into a porcelain pan, on the range. Let this stand a few minutes, then add the flour, which thoroughly mix together; then put in the yolks of two eggs, nutmeg, salt and pepper; then the milk and broth, putting a little at a time. Set this on the stove and let cook for several minutes, or until it thickens. Chop the chicken very fine, or what is better, put it in a machine, which will grind it as it should be. Squeeze a little lemon juice over the meat, and then pour on the sauce and set away on ice to cool. After it is thoroughly cold divide into croquettes. Beat the remaining yolks of eggs and add cracker dust, roll the croquettes in this mixture and drop into boiling lard.

Mrs. F. Ashton Henry.

CHICKEN CROQUETTES.

ONE chicken, one pair of sweet-breads, two ounces, of butter, one wine-glassful of cream, one loaf of stale bakers' bread, two eggs, red and black pepper, salt, parsley, grated onion, curry powder sufficient. Boil the chicken and sweet-breads separately until tender, saving the broth; chop together very fine. Season with red and black pepper and salt; add one teaspoonful of grated onion, grate the bread into crumbs until the bulk equals two-thirds of the bulk of meat. Mix the crumbs and meat, and moisten with warmed broth until it adheres to the spoon. Heat the cream to boiling, melt the butter in it, and add to the mixture. When all is sufficiently cool, add the eggs (beating whites and yolks together). Now add curry and parsley and, if necessary, more salt and pepper, until the seasoning is satisfactory. Put the mass on ice for a few hours, then mould into forms, and set them on ice again for two hours. Dip in egg, roll in crumbs and boil in lard.

Mrs. J. M. Harry.

FISH CROQUETTES.

TWO pounds of cold fish, one-quarter of a pound of butter, one tablespoonful of flour, one-quarter of a pint of milk; pepper and salt to taste; parsley, grated nutmeg to taste, two eggs. Mince the fish very fine, carefully removing all bones and skin. Melt the butter in a sauce pan and stir in gradually the flour, and the milk, boiling hot; pepper, salt and nutmeg, and a little chopped parsley. Stir all this over the fire until it thickens, then add the fish, and let it cook a few minutes, stirring all the time; then turn out on a dish to cool. Make the fish into balls and dip into the beaten eggs, then into fine bread crumbs. When all made up, dip again in eggs and crumbs. Fry in boiling lard till brown.

Mrs. Hayes.

OYSTER CROQUETTES.

TWENTY-FIVE large oysters boiled until they begin to curl at the edges, drain off the liquor, saving one teacupful for the dressing. Chop the oysters fine. One teacupful of cream, two tablespoonfuls of butter and two tablespoonfuls of flour. Mix the flour and butter together. When melted, add cream gradually; to this add scant tablespoonful of *finely* chopped parsley; salt, cayenne pepper, and one egg well beaten. Boil one minute, take from the fire and add the oysters. Mix well together. Put on ice till *very cold*. Then form into croquettes. Roll in egg and bread crumbs. Let stand fifteen minutes, and drop in *boiling* lard.

DRESSING FOR OYSTER CROQUETTES.

One cupful of oyster liquor, two tablespoonfuls of butter, two tablespoonfuls of flour (slightly browned). Beat the flour and butter well together, and stir in the liquor, which has been boiled and skimmed; pepper, salt and pinch of finely chopped parsley. Pour this over croquettes just before serving.

Mrs. Jno. M. Rogers.

OYSTER CROQUETTES.

LET one quart of oysters come to a boil; drain off the juice and chop fine; add one egg, one-half bunch of chopped parsley, a piece of butter size of an egg, one-half cupful of cream, one-half of small onion, red pepper and salt, bread crumbs enough to hold them together. Mould and roll in crumbs, set away to harden before frying.

Mrs. Hayes.

POTATO CROQUETTES.

SEASON cold mashed potatoes with pepper, salt and nutmeg; add one tablespoonful of butter to every cupful of potatoes, then beat to a cream. Bind with two beaten eggs; add some minced parsley. Roll into oval balls, dip in beaten eggs, then in bread crumbs, and fry in hot lard.

Mrs. J. P. Wickersham.

CHICKEN CROQUETTES.

ONE chicken, boiled and chopped fine; two tablespoonfuls of flour and two tablespoonfuls of butter, mix together; one-half pint of cream. Boil cream and stir flour into it. A little chopped parsley and grated onion to taste. Mould them, dip in bread crumbs, then in egg, then in crumbs and put in moulds and fry.

S. C. Dye.

RULES FOR CANNING FRUITS.

APPLES, sour, boil ten minutes, six ounces of sugar per pound.

Pears, small and sour, boil thirty minutes, eight ounces of sugar per pound.

Pears, Bartlett, boil twenty minutes, six ounces of sugar per pound.

Cherries, boil five minutes, six ounces of sugar per pound.

Raspberries, boil six minutes, four ounces of sugar per pound.

Plums, boil ten minutes, six ounces of sugar per pound.

Blackberries, boil six minutes, six ounces of sugar per pound.

Strawberries, boil eight minutes, eight ounces of sugar per pound.

Whortleberries, boil five minutes, four ounces of sugar per pound.

Pie-plant, sliced, boil ten minutes, ten ounces of sugar per pound.

Peaches, whole, boil fifteen minutes, four ounces of sugar per pound.

Peaches, halves, boil eight minutes, four ounces of sugar per pound.

Crab Apples, whole, boil twenty-five minutes, eight ounces of sugar per pound,

Currants, ripe, boil six minutes, eight ounces of sugar per pound.

Grapes, boil ten minutes, eight ounces of sugar per pound.

Tomatoes, boil twenty minutes.

Pine Apples, sliced, one-half inch thick, boil fifteen minutes, six ounces of sugar per pound.

Gooseberries, boil eight minutes, four ounces of sugar per pound.

BEVERAGES.

EGG NOG.

ONE quart of rich cream, one pint of new milk, one dozen of eggs, one pound of sugar, one bottle of Jamaica, or New England rum, one bottle of California or French brandy. Separate yolks of eggs from the whites; reserving whites to be beaten lightly; add to yolks the sugar, and beat vigorously for one-half hour, until *very light;* then add, alternately, the rum and brandy, *slowly,* a cupful at a time. After it is thoroughly incorporated, add the cream and milk, and lastly, the beaten whites of the eggs.

Mrs. Wm. Hearne.
Wheeling, W. Va.

BLACKBERRY CORDIAL.

TO two quarts of blackberry juice, add one pound of loaf sugar, one-half ounce of nutmeg, one-half ounce of cinnamon, one-quarter ounce of allspice, one-quarter ounce of cloves. Boil all together for a short time, and when cold, add one pint of brandy. Strain and bottle it.

Mrs. J. L. Burtnett.

GRAPE WINE.

PUT ripe grapes into a tub, mash well with a potato masher. To every gallon, pour over one quart of boiling water. Let stand for two or three days, no longer if the weather is warm. Strain off the juice well, and to every gallon, add three pounds of white sugar. Put into jugs and stop loosely until done working; then bottle it off and stop closely. To make good wine, grapes should hang longer on the vine.

E. S. Winslow.

GRANDMOTHER'S WHIPS.

SWEETEN one quart of cream to taste, and flavor with wine; whip with a whip churn. To be served in glasses with a slice of pound cake.

Mrs. A. P. Eves.

ELDER BLOSSOM WINE.

TO one quart of picked-off elder blossoms, take one gallon of water. Let water come to a boil, and add four pounds of sugar. When this comes to a boil pour over blossoms, which have been placed in an earthen crock. Let stand until cool, and add one sliced lemon, white of one egg, beaten to a light froth, and two tablespoonfuls of home-made yeast. Let stand three days, then strain and place in cellar to ferment, skimming every three or four days. When done fermenting, place in bottles, and air tight. Ready for use in six weeks.

Mrs. J. D. Burtnett.

RASPBERRY VINEGAR.

PUT one quart of vinegar to two quarts of mashed raspberries. Let stand in the sun one day. The next day strain through a jelly bag, and add two more quarts of berries. The day following strain again, and to five quarts of juice add one pint of water. Let it boil up with the addition of one and one-half pints of fresh vinegar, and six pounds of sugar.

Mary S. Benn.

GRAPE WINE.

PUT the fruit through a wine-press, and after all has been pressed, take the pulp and pour a little boiling water over it; then press the juice from that, and mix it with the pure juice. Measure and allow three pounds of sugar to a gallon of the juice. Mix well and set away to ferment, keeping some out to fill up the jug every morning. In about six weeks cork up and set away until about Christmas. Then it can be racked off into bottles.

Mrs. A. P Evey.

DINNER GIVING.

DINNER being the principal meal at which guests are entertained, a few practical hints as to the proper mode of its serving, will not be found out of place in connection with the directions given for its preparation.

Tables of any shape may be used, but the one best adapted for decorating and serving a well cooked dinner, is a round table of a size capable of conveniently seating six or eight persons (see cut), and particular care should be taken to have the chairs surrounding, all of equal height. The table should first be covered with a thick baize, or canton flannel, under a table cloth of fine linen damask, of spotless purity, thick enough and, at the same time, of such firmness of texture as to obviate the necessity of being starched. The napkins should correspond.

According to the taste of the hostess, many different kinds of ornaments may be used in decorating with silver, china and other ware, yet none are more beautiful or more expressive of refined taste than natural flowers. These may be used as a centrepiece in *épergnes* or vases; or in raised dishes, and can be trailed along the table, or festooned from the chandelier above. Even growing plants can be used in pots, when properly screened, and every plate should be graced by a small bouquet or a *boutonnière* of blossoms.

At each plate place as many knives, forks and spoons as will be used in the several courses—knives and spoons to the right, and forks to the left. Upon the plate lay an artistically folded napkin, and by its side a small "bread and butter plate," bearing a piece of bread or roll. This, with a filled glass of ice water, and as many kinds of wine glasses as there are different kinds of wine, if it be served, make up the equipment of each plate. Salt-cellars, pepper stands, cruets, etc., together with the necessary fancy spoons required in serving the various dishes, should be grouped at either end of the table, and upon which a few shallow dishes of garnished relishes should also be placed at intervals.

For the dinner, provide the necessary number of plates, placing all those required for cold dishes on the side table, having those intended for the dessert already prepared, each bearing a finger-bowl half filled with water and perfumed with a slice of lemon, a few violets or a geranium leaf. The effectiveness of the bowls can be vastly improved by enfolding them with lace or embroidered napkins, which guests, in using, should be careful not to soil. The salad bowl, the fruit stands, a reserved plate of bread and one of butter should also be placed on the side table.

When dinner is announced, the soup tureen must be found already in place in front of the hostess, who occupies the head of the table. The announcement should always be made verbally, never by the ringing of a bell, stroke of a gong or other noisy signal, and clocks should be banished from the dining room.

In serving the dinner, as well as seating the guests, there should be no hurry, no confusion, no anxiety whatever displayed, either on the part of the host or of hostess. No audible word should be spoken between them and the attendants, who are expected to have been already fully instructed as to their duties, the routine of which is very simple.

In bringing the various courses to table, the soup, salad and dessert should always be placed before the hostess, all other dishes before the host. Before bringing them in, the pile of plates necessary for their service should be placed immediately before the host or hostess, as the case may be, and the course dish deposited in front. When each plate is ready the host puts it on the attendant's salver, who places it, *with his own hand*, before the guest, and in a similar manner, before each of the guests. Upon other dishes of the same course, the attendant will place a spoon, and then present it at the left side of each person, who is expected to help himself.

As soon as any one has finished with his plate, it should be at once removed without waiting for the others to finish, and when all have been so removed, the next course should follow immediately. The same method will be followed with all the courses up to the dessert. After serving which, the attendant will leave the room, his duties for the time being having ended.

This method of serving dinner is so simple, and attended with so little ceremony, that it would be well for all families to practice it daily. It is absolutely methodical and is as equally adapted to the ordinary routine life, as it is—with the addition of a few waiters—to the most elaborate of dinner parties, for giving which the servants thus become thoroughly trained. Besides this, we all know that a well served dinner not only improves the taste of its dishes, but invariably arouses a spirit of pride and emulation in the cook, which secures its better and more healthful preparation.

There are a few general rules for better guidance, to be observed in dinner-giving, which may be summarized as follows:

Never over supply a table, nor overload a plate, nor importune a guest to be rehelped.

Have the dishes few in number, but perfect of the kind.

Let the flowers be fresh, and the linen dazzlingly white.

Have the plates properly warmed, and the wines properly tempered.

Never show the least anxiety, hurry or worry, whatever contretemps, disappointment or accident may occur.

Arrange the seats of the guests before entering the dining room, so as to avoid any confusion in seating.

If the guest to be honored be a lady, seat her at the right hand of the host, if a gentleman, on the right of the hostess.

In seating guests, so arrange as to bring congenial people into contact.

In dinners of over eight guests, place a small card bearing the name of each person at his or her plate.

If the company be larger, "menu cards" are in order, printed or painted for the occasion. Pretty designs for which, are to be found in abundance, and purchased at a trifling cost.

There is no rigid rule as to the order of serving at table. Where there is a single attendant, the lady guest, seated at the right of the host, or the most elderly lady present, should be first served.

As soon as the second person is helped, there should be no further waiting before eating.

The hostess invariably gives the signal for rising by pushing back her chair, when all rise and remain standing until the ladies have left the room.

Cigars are then served, if served at all.

Coffee may be served either as a finality with the dessert at the table, or subsequently by attendants in the drawing room. The former custom being preferable.

The foregoing embodies only a few hints respecting the hospitable art of dinner-giving, but there is a wide scope for the display of individuality, originality and good taste in choosing the dishes and decorations of the table. The opportunities vary with the seasons, the viands and the company to be honored, and often call for the exercise of a judgment, invention and refinement akin to genius.

It is hardly necessary to allude to dining invitations, further than to state that, as in serving a dinner, true refinement is best displayed by the simplicity with which the preliminaries are conducted. When not *en famille*, invitations should be extended by a written card, stating, briefly, that

Mrs. Robinson requests the pleasure of Mr. Brown's company, on Wednesday evening, June 5, at six o'clock.
R. S. V. P.

The person invited should respond, without delay, by messenger—never by post. If he declines, it is in the following terms:

Mr. Brown regrets that a previous engagement prevents the acceptance of Mrs. Robinson's kind invitation for Wednesday evening.

If he accepts:

Mr. Brown accepts, with pleasure, Mrs. Robinson's invitation for Wednesday evening.

On the appointed day, the guest should make it a point to arrive at ten minutes before the hour specified, but, under no circumstances, to arrive later than the hour appointed. On the other hand, from five to ten minutes is the extreme limit a hostess can be expected to await the arrival of a dilatory guest. EDI.

THE TABLE.

INVALIDS' FARE.

SOMETHING with which to coax the appetite of the convalescent or semi-invalid, is often a perplexing question. Herein is given a few recipes which have been long tried and tested.

All will agree that it is not only what is offered to the invalid, but the careful nicety of preparing and setting forth, that is of the utmost importance; for we all know how trifles affect us, when ill. Let us then look first to the tray and its accompaniments; a lacquered wooden Japanese tray is to be preferred to the old-fashioned metal ones, on account of lightness, and freedom from "clatter." Have a tiny sugar-bowl and creamer for the tray, which are very convenient, as well as an addition to the dainty appearance; these may be bought of some pretty ware or glass for a trifle. If one is the happy possessor of a tiny tête-à-tête set, or one of the small old-fashioned cut-glass sets, so much the better.

Of course the linen and china for the tray should be *sans reproche*, and a little careful forethought will always select the cup and the plate that the invalid is known to be fond of. "Things taste so much better out of pretty dishes." A bit of scarlet geranium, with a leaf, or a spray of some pretty flower in a tiny specimen vase, is a dainty addition, and welcomed by the weary invalid.

The following few recipes will be found practical and useful.

SIMPLE WINE JELLY.—One-half box of gelatine, one tablespoonful of powdered gum-arabic, one pint of port wine; put all in a jug, cover with white paper, and let stand two hours; then put all in a porcelain lined sauce pan, bring to a boil, strain, pour in mould, and cool. Cut in tiny pieces to serve.

RENNET WINE FOR MAKING CUSTARD.—Clean and dry three inches of calf rennet, put it into a pint of sherry, and set away to use. Three tablespoonfuls will be enough to curdle a quart of milk.

RENNET CUSTARD.—To one quart of warm milk add three tablespoonfuls of rennet wine, and five teaspoonfuls of sugar; flavor if wished. Care should be taken to have the milk not hot, but warm.

ARROWROOT CUSTARD.—One tablespoonful of arrowroot, one egg, one pint of milk, one tablespoonful of sugar. Mix the arrowroot to a paste with a little of the cold milk; put the remainder of the milk in a porcelian-lined sauce pan; when it boils, stir in the arrowroot, egg and sugar well beaten together, stir and cool.

BOUILLON.—Five pounds of juicy beef cut in small pieces, and simmered slowly for two and one-half hours, in two quarts of water. Remove every bit of fat, strain through a cloth, season with salt, no pepper.

CODFISH.—Cut in tiny pieces a piece of codfish, and pour over it boiling water, to freshen it; pour off the water, add some cream. This is nice poured over toast.

SEA-MOSS BLANCMANGE.—Wash thoroughly a cup of Irish moss. Put a quart of milk in a porcelain-lined sauce pan, and add the moss; when the milk is well thickened, strain and cool. It can be served with powdered sugar; or sugar, cream, and a bit of fruit jelly. This will be found nutritious, and acceptable to the most sensitive stomach.

TOAST-WATER and tamarind water were drinks highly valued in illness by our grandmothers. Toast-water is made by putting pieces of toasted bread in a glass jar, and covering the pieces with water. When the water is colored, it is ready to drink. To prepare tamarind water, put a cupful of tamarinds in a quart of cold water, and let it stand a day, then strain.

PANADA was an invalid delicacy highly valued fifty years ago, and will be found nourishing and palatable. It is made by boiling together for three minutes one glassful of wine and three glassfuls of water; add a teaspoonful of lemon juice, one cupful of grated bread crumbs; boil one minute then serve. A grating of nutmeg will add to the flavor, but it is not advised for an invalid.

TOAST can be made to look tempting by cutting off the crust of the slice, cutting out the crumb with a tiny cake-cutter, then toasting.

NEVER add pepper or other spices to food for an invalid, and use as little butter—it is needless to say, that of the best quality—as possible.

Introduction to the Sick Room.

THERE is a peculiar knack, as one might call it, in waiting upon the sick. No one is so quick to detect the want of aptitude as the sufferer, and if the latter has taken a dislike to the nurse, it is better for her to retire until the aversion has dissipated itself.

The dislike may be but a whimsical fancy, and yet is as injurious as if based upon abundant cause. The hand of one watcher, toying gently with the hair of the sick one, will woo to slumber with its soothing touch; the hand of another may irritate and induce increased wakefulness.

There is no time when love lends such a charm to every word and action as in the hour of sickness; and yet there is no time when a young girl is made more conscious of her insufficiency of the fact that she is almost as helpless as the invalid.

The mother generally knows, through experience, how to nurse her sick daughter; but very often the daughter does not know how to nurse her sick mother. She fails for want of method and a knowledge of what ought to be done and how it ought to be done. She becomes agitated when she ought to be calm; she becomes irritated when she ought to be serene; her patience becomes exhausted just when it is most needed.

Nursing does not merely consist in suiting food to a taste which illness has made ten times more fastidious than usual, or in giving the proper medicine in proper quantities at proper intervals, or in bathing the languid head, or in moving the weary body. There is a delicacy; besides delicacy of food and delicacy of touch. It includes the modulation of the voice, the movements about the room, the suppression of needless noises, and a score of other things of the kind.

The young nurse should seem cheerful and hopeful though she does not feel so. Indications of alarm and distress must be suppressed. The dress should not rattle or the shoes creak. The movements to and fro should be gentle and unobtrusive. Nothing should be said that the patient ought not to hear, for in sickness the hearing is often unnaturally quickened.

Rejected dainties should not be allowed to remain in the room under the delusion that they will be fancied by-and-by. It is a certain way of making the patient loathe the food.

In shaking up a pillow do it with the utmost gentleness. To raise the invalid to a sitting posture, put a scarf or long shawl behind the pillow and let two persons each take an end and gently draw up the patient.

No medicine is so beneficial to the sick as fresh air. It is the most reviving of all cordials if administered with prudence. Doors and windows should not be thrown open suddenly or at random. Fresh air should be let into the room gradually, and, if possible, by opening the windows of an adjoining apartment. If the windows of the patient's room cannot be opened, a good plan is to swing the door quickly backwards and forwards.

Muslin rags soaked in aromatic vinegar, and suspended near the door, so as to be agitated by the draught, will prevent unpleasant smells and purify the air. Rags dipped in chloride of lime, and suspended across the room on a cord are a disinfectant in cases of fever.

As books of instruction for nurses, may not be within the reach of every young girl, it will be well for her to note these practical hints.

Household Hints.

MIXTURE FOR WASHING FLANNELS.

TWO bars of Ivory soap, four and one-half gallons of soft water, two ounces of borax, ammonia enough to give it a strong smell. Use a cupful of the preparation in tepid water when washing flannels. It will remove all dirt, and the flannels will not shrink.

ONION ODORS.

WHEN cooking onions, set a tin cupful of vinegar on the stove, and let it boil, and, it is said, you will smell no disagreeable odor.

DETERGENT.

ONE and one-half ounces of white castile soap, four ounces of aqua ammonia, one ounce of ether, one ounce of alcohol. Shave the soap fine and heat in one pint of water until dissolved, then add two quarts more water, and all the ingredients. Bottle; keep tightly corked. Use wine-glassful in one pint of water.

MISCELLANEOUS.

STREW the store room shelves with a few cloves to drive away ants.

Ink spots, when fresh, may be removed by washing in sweet milk.

A little salt rubbed on a discolored egg spoon will remove the stains.

To freshen stale crackers, put them into a hot oven for a few minutes.

To prevent flour lumping, add a little salt before mixing with milk or water.

To clean brushes, dissolve a little borax or soda in water. Wash and dry quickly.

Camphor in drawers or trunks will prevent mice from doing injury to the contents.

To take out fruit stains, stretch the stained part over a bowl and pour on boiling water.

To keep cakes from sticking to a griddle, rub it with brown paper.

Lard is hot when a blue smoke arises from it.

For the Hair—Wash in cold sage tea.

Cocoa Butter—Apply at night to face and hands, and wash off in the morning. This is excellent for the skin, and keeps it soft and clear.

Ink Spots on Books—A solution of oxalic acid will remove them without injuring the print.

Berry Stains—The fumes of a brimstone match will remove berry stains from a book, paper or engraving.

For a tight, hoarse cough, where phlegm is not raised, or with difficulty, take *hot* water often, as hot as can be sipped. This will be found to give immediate and permanent relief.

www.ingramcontent.com/pod-product-compliance
Lightning Source LLC
Chambersburg PA
CBHW020830230426
43666CB00007B/1166